status and conformity

TIME
LIFE
BOOKS

ENCYCLOPAEDIA OF GARDENING
HUMAN BEHAVIOUR
THE GREAT CITIES
THE ART OF SEWING
THE OLD WEST
THE WORLD'S WILD PLACES
THE EMERGENCE OF MAN
LIFE LIBRARY OF PHOTOGRAPHY
FOODS OF THE WORLD
TIME-LIFE LIBRARY OF ART
GREAT AGES OF MAN
LIFE SCIENCE LIBRARY
LIFE NATURE LIBRARY
YOUNG READER'S LIBRARY

HUMAN BEHAVIOUR

status and conformity

BY RICHARD W. MURPHY

AND THE EDITORS OF TIME-LIFE BOOKS

TIME-LIFE INTERNATIONAL (NEDERLAND) B.V.

The Author: Richard W. Murphy is a freelance writer, based in Paris. A former music editor of TIME, he is also the author of the Cézanne volume in the TIME-LIFE Library of Art.

General Consultants for Human Behaviour: *Robert M. Krauss* is Professor of Psychology at Columbia University. He has taught at Princeton and Harvard and was Chairman of the Psychology Department at Rutgers. He is the co-author of *Theories in Social Psychology*, formerly edited the *Journal of Experimental Social Psychology* and contributes articles to many journals on aspects of human behaviour and social interaction.

Peter I. Rose, a specialist on racial and ethnic relations, is Sophia Smith Professor of Sociology and Anthropology at Smith College and is on the graduate faculty of the University of Massachusetts. His books include *They and We, The Subject is Race* and *Americans from Africa*. Professor Rose has also taught at Goucher, Wesleyan, Colorado, Clark, Yale, Amherst, the University of Leicester in England, Kyoto University in Japan and Flinders University in Australia.

James W. Fernandez is Professor of Anthropology at Princeton University. His field research has concentrated on cultural changes in East, West and South Africa, and the Iberian peninsula. He has been President of the Northeastern Anthropological Association and a consultant to the Foreign Service Institute. He has also taught at Dartmouth College.

Special Consultant for Status and Conformity: *Harry C. Bredemeier* is a Professor of Sociology at Douglass College at Rutgers, The State University of New Jersey. He is particularly interested in deviance and social control. He is the co-author of *The Analysis of Social Systems* and *Social Problems in America: Costs and Casualties of an Acquisitive Society*, and is co-editor of *Environments, People, and Inequalities: Some Current Problems*.

European Consultants: *Arthur H. Halsey* is Director of the Department of Social and Administrative Studies at Oxford and Professorial Fellow of Nuffield College. He has lectured at Chicago University, Harvard, and the London School of Economics, and was a Fellow at the Centre for Advanced Study of the Behavioural Sciences at Palo Alto. Professor Halsey is a frequent broadcaster on matters of social policy and education and has published widely in Europe and the United States.

Carl F. Graumann is Professor of Psychology and Director of the Psychological Institute at Heidelberg University. He has lectured at Bonn University, Duquesne University in Pittsburgh and the New School for Social Research in New York. Dr. Graumann was Chairman of the Deutsche Gesellschaft Fuer Psychologie and Editor-in-Chief of the handbook *Sozialpsychologie*. He is co-editor of *Zeitschrift Fuer Sozialpsychologie* and has published books on perspective, thinking and motivation.

Jos Jaspars is Professor of Social Psychology at the University of Leiden in the Netherlands. He is a member of the European Association for Experimental Social Psychology and an affiliate of the American Psychological Association. Professor Jaspars has taught at the University of Oslo, the University of Delaware in the United States and the University of Jakarta in Indonesia. He is editor of the journal, *Social Psychology*.

Serge Moscovici, sociologist and psychosociologist, teaches at Ecole Pratique des Hautes Etudes de Paris. He has made numerous researches in social psychosociology. His publications include: *Society Against Nature, Psychanalyse: Son Image et Son Public*, and *Hommes Domestiques et Hommes Sauvages*.

HUMAN BEHAVIOUR
Editorial Staff for *Status and Conformity*:
EDITOR: William K. Goolrick
Text Editors: Richard Craven, Betsy Frankel
Picture Editor: Adrian Allen
Designer: John Martinez
Associate Designer: Marion Flynn
Staff Writers: Carol Clingan, Susan Hillaby, Suzanne Seixas
Chief Researcher: Anne Morrison
Researchers: Karen Bates, Oscar Chiang, Barbara Fleming, Dunstan Harris.
Beatrice Hsia, Shirley Miller,
Gail Nussbaum, Heidi Sanford, Jane Sugden
Editorial Assistant: Janet Hubbard

EDITOR, EUROPEAN EDITION: Kit van Tulleken
Researcher: Milly Trowbridge
Designer: Graham Davis
Editorial Assistant: Krystyna Davidson

Valuable help was given by the following departments and individuals of Time Inc.: Editorial Production, Norman Airey; Library, Benjamin Lightman; Picture Collection, Doris O'Neil; Photographic Laboratory, George Karas; TIME-LIFE News Service, Murray J. Gart; Correspondents Ann Natanson and Deborah Sgardello (Rome), Margot Hapgood and Dorothy Bacon (London), Maria Vicenza Aloisi and Josephine du Brusle (Paris), Elisabeth Kraemer (Bonn), S. Chang and Frank Iwama (Tokyo), Tony Avirgan (Dar es Salaam), Mary Johnson (Stockholm), Felix Rosenthal (Moscow), James Shepherd (New Delhi).

Contents

The Social Order

1

In his novel *The Magic Mountain*, Thomas Mann described the social world of a Swiss tuberculosis sanatorium, basing his fictional setting on his own observations of an institution in which his wife was a patient. What struck Mann especially was the sanatorium's rigid hierarchy of social status, in which each incoming patient was classified quickly according to his level of importance. The system of stratification had nothing to do with money, talent, occupation, age or social background. It was dictated by the severity of illness. The patients who were nearest death were the aristocrats, while the milder cases were held to be socially inferior—not only by their fellow patients but even by themselves. Sometimes the mild cases got to feeling so worthless that they exaggerated their illnesses, adding a few tenths of a degree to their daily temperature readings in the hope that they would be able to gain admittance to the aristocracy.

It is easy to marvel at the strange values of a group that would confer honour on the basis of ill health. Yet the truth is that the patients in Mann's sanatorium in Switzerland were yielding to a universal impulse. For the mere fact of living together in groups causes people to sort one another out and assign more prestige and importance to some than to others. In every society throughout history individuals have been classified into categories that rate them as being inferior or superior to one another. One consequence of this process, which sociologists call social stratification, is that there has never been a society that was genuinely egalitarian. Inequality is as old as man. Most societies are stratified in a manner that resembles a ladder, with those people who are the most powerful and held in the highest esteem occupying the top rung, those who matter least—according to the society's standards—at the bottom, and all the rest ranged in order on the various rungs in between.

The criteria by which people are arrayed up and down the ladder may vary greatly from culture to culture, or even within a culture. These criteria may include occupation, religion, race, wealth, knowledge, age, sex, intelligence, good looks or a combination of these and many other factors. For example, Mr. Smith who lives at 113 Arlington Place may be a businessman or a cello player or a jockey or a judge. In addition, he may be a Catholic, a Protestant or a Muslim. He has a racial identification; he belongs to an age group; he is a son, and he may be a husband and father. He could be an alcoholic, and he could be the best weekend tennis player in Esher, Surrey. Each of these identifications carries with it a certain amount of weight, and the sum total of all of them helps to determine Mr. Smith's status, a term that sociologists use to connote his position on the ladder.

The effect of status upon a person's life is difficult to overrate. Beginning at an individual's birth and continuing right up to the time of his death, his status will play an important role in the development of his personality and will most likely dictate many of the options and choices that constitute his life style. However much men may speak of being born equal, the idea is more myth than reality. A child is automatically assigned at birth the position of his family in the social order. If his family is wealthy, for example, he will be treated with more deference than he would be if they were poor. But the matter does not end there. He will also occupy or acquire a whole complex of other status positions, which may change as his life unfolds. Along with his family status, he will have at the outset the status of a child rather than that of an adolescent or an adult. And very early on, he will probably learn that his status as a boy sets him apart from the girl children in his family. If he happens to have been born better-looking than his peers, that biological accident, too, will assign him a different status. And in the intensely competitive world of childhood, he will discover that even such an apparently inconsequential matter as an odd-sounding name can affect his standing among his fellows.

Moreover, as he grows older, he will find that his status will influence his politics, his choice of a marriage partner, the number of children he will have, his whole concept of reality and his manner of reacting to it. Studies conducted by American sociologist Melvin Kohn show that people who are low on the social scale consistently tend to feel they have little control over their lives, while those in higher brackets look upon life as something that can be moulded to their own wishes and needs. And in England, psychologist H. J. Eysenck found that the typical personality shaped by a life spent in a British working-class district was suspicious, secretive, conformist and intolerant of people and ideas outside the immediate surroundings. In fact, an expert knowing nothing more about a man than his position on the social scale can reconstruct with a reasonable degree of accuracy a profile of how he lives. According to sociologists Peter and Brigitte Berger, it is even possible to speculate on such intimate details as whether a man prefers to have the light on or off when he has sexual intercourse with his wife. (If he is an American of the upper-middle class, the light will probably be on.)

The individual who tries to improve his status may discover that the ladder is slippery, and that it is extremely difficult to gain a footing on a higher rung and extremely painful to drop lower. The dilemma of those who try to climb the ladder by changing their life styles was demonstrated in the 1933 film *Bombshell* by Jean Harlow, who portrayed a character trying to put on upper-class manners when she was addressing her butler. "Open the window a particle, James," said she, "and leave us breathe a little air."

The mental stress may be even greater when the movement is downwards. Psychologists conducted interviews with hundreds of Americans who had lost their jobs during the 1974-1975 economic slump and found that they were suffering not only from economic anxiety but also from a feeling of worthlessness. The loss of self-esteem they experienced manifested itself in diverse and sometimes bizarre ways—total apathy, outbursts of anger that were apparently unmotivated, bouts of heavy drinking, episodes of wife- or child-beating, sudden ruptures of old friendships. The investigators concluded that the loss of a sense of identity as a functioning and therefore useful member of society was actually more crippling than the loss of a steady income.

S ocial stratification is not confined to human beings, of course, but is a characteristic of most creatures that live in groups. Ants and bees have very complex hierarchical organizations. Mammals have leaders and followers, dominant males and females. When a herd of cattle goes out to pasture or comes back through the gate into the farmyard, one cow serves as the leader and the others follow behind. Wolves have a finely developed dominance hierarchy. A subordinate wolf will go through life without mating if it cannot find a female that has been unclaimed by a superior male.

The dominance system is more sophisticated among the primates. Baboons have a well-established hierarchy of dominant males. The leaders of a troop of baboons exert a clear line of authority over other members. Whenever fighting breaks out, they will step in and break it up. The females treat them with deference, grooming them frequently and sitting beside them. When food is tossed to baboons, a dominant male will take it and no subordinate will make a move to touch it. Even in sleeping, the dominant males play the role of leader. Baboons range over wide areas during the day. They are terrified of the dark,

and sleep high in the tops of the trees, where they are safe from snakes and carnivores. The dominant males designate the trees in which the troop will spend the night.

Chimpanzees, which are the animals most closely related to man, live in male-ruled societies. The males maintain their superiority through physical attacks or through intimidation—they will charge along the ground, hurl rocks and drag branches, leap up and down, and bend saplings. Jane Goodall, the ethologist who lived with chimpanzees in Tanzania, told of one she called Mike that would bang empty oil cans together to frighten the other members of the group and thus was able to maintain its superior status. Goodall also reported that the animals tend to show deference to the dominant members of their groups in their greetings. "Chimpanzees may kiss, touch or pat one another, hold hands or embrace," she wrote. "A male may chuck a female or an infant under the chin. Gestures of this sort indicate the relevant social status of the individuals concerned and undoubtedly serve to re-affirm the subordinate chimpanzee's continuing acknowledgement of the other's superior status." There is even stratification among female chimpanzees and their young: The older females are deferred to by the other females and young males.

Animal dominance systems are based on physical strength, aggression and threats of aggression. The stratification that exists in modern human societies is much more subtle and much more complex. Stratification goes back to the dawn of civilization in the great river valleys of the Middle East. Before then people had grouped themselves together in roving bands in which the sorcerer outranked the hunter, and all of the work duties involved in providing and caring for the family were divided between men and women. But it was only when people began to form permanent settlements along the banks of the Tigris, the Euphrates, the Nile and the Indus, that complex economic organizations and truly stratified societies began to emerge.

Ancient Egypt is a fine example of a highly stratified early civilization. Egyptian society, appropriately enough, was formed like a pyramid, with the pharaoh at the apex and the masses of humble peasants at the base. The pharaoh was the incarnation of the gods and the personification of the state. He was perceived as responsible for the rise and fall of the Nile, the crop yield and the fortunes of the state both in war and peace. He was respected and revered, and lived in a splendid palace with broad courts and frescoed halls, where shaven-headed priests and other dignitaries came and went. His chief administrative officer was the vizier, a man possessing great prestige, who held dozens of titles, including those of prince, count and seal bearer and was the sole

11

companion to the king. The vizier presided over the highest court and supervised the collection of taxes, and he was the minister of war, the chief of police and the director of public works.

The priests were organized into a hierarchy that was finely stratified. Only a small and select number of them were permitted to enter the sanctuary of the temple, and only the high priest himself was permitted to break open the seals that secured the sanctuary doors. Ranged beneath the high priest and his immediate inferiors were other priests who served as astrologers, scholars, readers of the sacred texts, singers and musicians. Still others, further down the ladder of the priestly society, were the bearers of sacred objects and the overseers of the temple artisans.

Beneath the priests came the professional soldiers, bureaucrats, magistrates, scribes, artisans, unskilled labourers, peasants and slaves, in that order. Positions in this society were largely hereditary, with the exceptions of those of the soldiers and scribes. Either of these positions

The last British viceroy of India, Lord Mountbatten, poses with his family and some of the 5,000 household servants who helped him maintain his position. Even the servants were stratified from top to bottom—for example, the 418 gardeners were aided by 50 assistants charged with keeping birds out of the gardens.

could be inherited but their ranks were also open to any man of talent, regardless of the place that he occupied by virtue of his birth.

Egypt was but one of many highly stratified civilizations of the past. India gave the world a rigid caste system in which lineage sharply defined status and behaviour. The feudal order that existed in mediaeval Europe divided people into three estates: the prestigious nobility, the clergy and the townspeople (peasants were not included in the reckoning). The feudal system finally ended, in a technical sense, with the French Revolution, but it had become outmoded and unwieldy long before the Revolution.

The expansion of trade that began during the Renaissance and accelerated wildly with the Industrial Revolution radically changed the entire structure of the status ladder in Western culture. It brought several new classes of businessmen, professionals and craftsmen, whose importance to their society demanded that there be a complete redistribution of power, prestige and wealth.

The Industrial Revolution also had significant side effects. "Prior to the coming of the Industrial Revolution," commented sociologist Harold Hodges, "those of top and bottom rank, and to a lesser extent those of middling rank, had each been characterized by distinctive styles of life: dress, speech, manners, education, recreation, and leisure-time pursuits varied sharply from level to level. One could tell at a glance who 'belonged' where." Suddenly that situation of clear distinctions changed as improvements in the production and distribution of goods and services enabled most people to enjoy things that previously had been limited to a fortunate few.

While the differences between ranks are not so obvious nowadays, they have become more numerous and complex. All but the simplest of societies now have not one but many systems of stratification existing side by side and influencing one another. Mr. Smith, whose place on the status ladder was set by his occupation, religion and tennis skill, among other things, might find that the ladder itself changed with geography. His attributes might give him high rank at home in suburban Esher, but count for little on the different ladder of urban and cosmopolitan London, even though it is only 16 kilometres away. On the other hand, an individual may seem less consequential at home than elsewhere. The author William Faulkner was written off as a harmless eccentric by most of his fellow citizens in Oxford, Mississippi, but in the larger world he was so esteemed that he won one of the highest accolades of his profession—the Nobel Prize for Literature.

Each factor that contributes to an individual's general status may be more than a unitary element to be weighed; it may turn out to consist of a whole status ladder of its own. Every occupation or group, for example, seems to establish a status system for itself. In the autobiographical book *Down and Out in Paris and London*, George Orwell describes the astonishment he felt when he discovered the rigid system of stratification that exists among kitchen employees in a finely organized first-class hotel. Hired as a dishwasher, Orwell innocently showed up for his first day of work wearing a moustache and was roundly berated by the manager. "Shave that moustache off at once!" Orwell was told. "*Nom de Dieu*, who ever heard of a *plongeur* with a moustache?" Later he found out that "waiters in good hotels do not wear moustaches, and to show their superiority they decree that *plongeurs* shall not wear them either; and the cooks wear their moustaches to show their contempt for the waiters." Orwell concluded: "A cook or waiter was as much above a *plongeur* as a captain above a private."

Within a particular society, the status systems of special groups may be completely at variance with the status system at large. Prostitutes, for instance, rank low in the social scale in almost all Western societies. Yet a number of studies have shown that prostitutes have their own rigid hierarchy, which ranges from high-class call girl to common street-walker. The fee a prostitute can command, her clothes, her address and her political connections all help to define her professional status. So does the style in which she can afford to keep her pimp. In fact, says Harold Greenwald in a well-known study of call girls, successful prostitutes lavish gifts on their pimps for the same reason that successful business-men give expensive presents to their wives—to signify high status.

In America, stratification systems are further multiplied by con-siderations of ethnic origin. Thus, a wealthy banker who is white and Protestant will have his status in his occupational hierarchy reinforced by the high status of his race and religion, whereas a wealthy black banker will find his racial position to be in conflict with the status to which his occupation entitles him.

The situation of black Americans is well known, but there are other, less obvious examples of multiple standards of stratification in the United States. Many European readers are baffled by biographies of John F. Kennedy that discuss the former President's barely concealed social insecurities. In French eyes, for example, Kennedy was a man of unassailable status, by reason of his political position, considerable wealth, education, good looks and marriage to a beautiful, well-born woman. Yet Kennedy was the descendant of Irish Catholics who had recently emigrated to America, and his childhood was shaped by the pattern of religious and ethnic discrimination in his birthplace of Boston that had closed doors of social and professional advancement to Irish Catholics.

The multiplicity of stratification systems becomes more obvious when attention is turned from analysis of a single society to comparisons between societies. Almost every culture has a scheme of its own by which it allocates prestige and power. In addition the criteria for status in a society change with time so that the same attributes that contri-buted to the lofty position of great-grandfather may be a liability to his great-grandchildren.

The only measure of status that seems to be constant everywhere is sex. In every culture that scientists have observed, men outrank women; there are no Amazons, and apparently never were. Wealth, too, seems almost everywhere to confer status, although the Kwakiutl Indian chiefs of the Pacific Northwest Coast actually achieved high status by burning or destroying their worldly possessions. But even there, wealth was the criterion that determined rank—the ones with the greatest amount of wealth to destroy gained the highest prestige.

Back-combing their hair stylishly before mirrors they have brought along on a camping trip to Yosemite National Park, three young women succumb to one of the strongest human pressures: the need to conform to the behaviour of their peers.

Aside from the universal constants of sex and possibly wealth, the ladders of different cultures may differ so much that what brings honour in one is an embarrassment in another. Americans, for example, are generally upset if their children are shy, because shyness in America is a social liability. Yet the Japanese consider it a social asset. In a recent study of shyness in several countries that was conducted by Stanford University psychologists, two-thirds of the Japanese interviewed said they were shy, and though they did not enjoy being shy, felt that it enhanced their social positions. In Japan such a lack of assertiveness is admired. Similarly, the British have traditionally been known for a quality of imperturbability in the face of danger that mystifies others but is valued highly in Britain. One illustration of this British peculiarity is attributed to Richard Moggart, for many years a member of the British Foreign Service. Moggart used to try to illustrate the typical British imperturbability at diplomatic parties with a story of the famous exchange between the Duke of Wellington and his cavalry commander, the Earl of Uxbridge, at the battle of Waterloo:

Uxbridge: By God, I've lost my leg.

Wellington: So you have.

Moggart claimed that he never had any success in his telling of the anecdote, because the quality of not making a fuss, esteemed by the British, struck his listeners as a response that was totally unfeeling, if not downright lunatic.

Perhaps more important to the structure and operation of a culture are differences in the status that is accorded to age. In most Western societies, for example, old people have low status, chiefly because they are no longer biologically or economically productive. But there are societies in which old age automatically confers the highest rank in the community. This is true in rural China, where the family is still a large and close-knit unit, and where the elderly are regarded as the repositories of family history—as well as the possessors of accumulated wisdom. It is also true in the West African state of Dahomey, where the old are revered not only for their wisdom but also because they will soon be ancestral spirits—in which position they will exercise enormous influence over the daily fortunes of the tribe.

In other societies it is youth that enjoys high status. In French Polynesia, for example, the young outrank their parents. The tribe is conceived as "an upward growing, outward pushing tree," whose future is more important than its past. Thus, it is children—the new generation—who possess the greatest *mana*, or spiritual power, and their parents defer to them. Anthropologist Ralph Linton reported seeing a tribal chieftain in the Marquesas Islands who had been ousted from his home by his nine-year-old son. The two had had an argument, and the son had then used his *mana* to put a taboo on his father's house, compelling the father to move outside until the taboo was removed.

The value of many other attributes and actions varies as markedly around the world. While suicide is condemned in most societies, among the Japanese kamikaze pilots of the Second World War the act that was most valued was suicide. Individual excellence is rewarded in most societies, but the Zuñi Indians of New Mexico downgrade any member of the tribe who displays a personal achievement. When a Zuñi man has the bad grace to habitually win the tribal foot races, he is barred from further running competitions. Moreover, sociologists and anthropologists have long known that the behaviour thought to be aberrant in one setting may be esteemed in another; a person considered a madman in one society may be honoured elsewhere. Thus, the Mafia assassin, a psychopath in the eyes of the world, may in fact be revered within his own community, where men are valued for their strong-arm techniques and family loyalty. Similarly, the bombast honoured among the Kwakiutl Indians, which seems heartless and megalomaniacal to outsiders, was a measure of a man's worth to the Kwakiutl. Here, for example, is a 19th-century Kwakiutl chieftain's hymn to himself—one that was guaranteed to humiliate his rivals:

This is the cause of my laughter,
The cause of my laughter at the one who is hard up,
The one who points about for his ancestors that are chiefs,
The puny ones have no ancestors who were chiefs,
The puny ones have no names coming from their grandfathers,
The puny ones who work,
The puny ones who work hard,
Who make mistakes, who come from insignificant places in the world.
This only is the cause of my laughter.

The criteria that guarantee high status in one society may be so special that they are unknown elsewhere. The term WASP—an acronym for white Anglo-Saxon Protestant—is a good example. For a long time it connoted the ethnic and religious background from which America's ruling class was drawn. Yet when Elliot Richardson, then the newly appointed American Ambassador to Britain, was described as a WASP by an American taking part in a panel discussion on French television, the French members of the panel were bewildered. Though the American was able to explain what the word meant, and his co-panelists were able to understand the fact that generations of Americans considered it advantageous to come from a particular racial, ethnic and religious

Sporting a brand-new bra along with her beads and headdress, a young New Guinea woman incongruously tries to conform to Western notions rather than adhere to her own culture's customs.

background, he was utterly unable to convey the emotions of disdain, envy and resentment the word generated in the minds of various other American groups.

Within any one culture, the stratification system is under almost continuous remodelling, so that behaviour that has been honoured at one time is not necessarily honoured at another time. When Japanese novelist Yukio Mishima committed suicide in 1970 by ritually disembowelling himself, he was conforming to an ancient Samurai tradition that requires that a man have the courage to take his own life if he fails to fulfil his duty. But alas, Mishima's act could no longer capture the sympathies of modern Japan. This kind of tragedy, that of the man whose standards belong to another day, also was the inspiration for one of the great portraits of literature, Cervantes' Don Quixote, the extravagant Spanish gentleman whose misfortune it was to have aspirations of being a perfect knight long after the tradition of knighthood had passed from the earth.

On the other hand, there are many celebrated individuals who achieved high status in their own time but would probably seem to be disturbed personalities today. Modern scholars studying the 17th-century New England witchcraft trials have concluded, for example, that it was probably the prestigious Puritan divines responsible for the trials, not the people on trial, who had pathological tendencies. And psychologists think that many of the people in mediaeval monastic orders —who experienced visions, mortifications and spiritual ecstasies—might now be considered candidates for mental institutions. Similarly, in many primitive societies, the shaman, sorcerer or witch doctor often displayed what psychologists call hysterical tendencies; but in that setting at that time children who possessed these tendencies were carefully nurtured, for the behaviour conferred high status. The same has been true of epilepsy. Many heroes in pre-Islamic Arabian literature were apparently epileptics, whose seizures were thought to signify contact with the supernatural. In ancient Greece there was still another standard: Homer's hero Odysseus was held in high esteem partly for his cleverness as a liar and thief.

Since there seems to be no universal logic to the standards of stratification systems, the reasons for their continued existence has stirred debate among scholars for thousands of years, to say nothing of violence among ordinary folk who are bent on changing them. The dispute is three-cornered. Some philosophers argue that stratification is simply the result of conflicts among individuals and should not, therefore, be necessary in a properly organized society. Opposing that view is the claim that stratification is essential to the survival of a society because it assigns functions to the most qualified people. And then there are those who accept stratification but think an existing system is wrong and ought to be modified.

Plato proposed in *The Republic* that the status system of ancient Greece ought to be destroyed and replaced with one providing for communal ownership of all property. Plato was not opposed to social inequality per se. Indeed he believed that a ruling class was essential —so long as its members were chosen for their moral virtue and their intellect. This sweetly seductive idea of an intellectual aristocracy has had an irresistible appeal for social critics from Plato right up to Bertrand Russell.

Even Christianity, seemingly so egalitarian in its approach to social problems, has been of two minds about the evils and benefits of stratification. The very earliest Christian tradition contained a strong streak of radical socialism and advocated a classless egalitarianism, in part because its converts were drawn from the depressed classes of the Roman world. When Pliny the Younger warned the Emperor Trajan of "this contagious superstition", he was expressing alarm not at the spiritual content of Christianity, about which he knew little, but rather at its iconoclastic social ideas, which he viewed as posing a threat to the existing social structure of the Roman Empire. On the other hand, the letters of St. Peter and St. Paul are thoroughly conservative in cast. Both men believed in a rigid traditional structure; they defended the system of slavery, stressed the obedience that every slave owed his master, and implied that this social hierarchy had been ordained by God.

As Christianity became older, the official position of the Christian church became steadily more conservative in its support of the existing rigid stratification along aristocratic lines. In the 12th century, John of Salisbury, an English bishop, compared society to the human body and referred to the prince as the head and the common people as the feet. He also suggested that a society could only function properly when "the higher members shield the lower, and the lower respond faithfully and fully in like measure to the just demands of their superiors". However, within the church there were rebels. The Franciscans in the Roman Catholic Church and the Protestant Waldensians made a point of criticizing special privilege and extolling the virtues of poverty. In fact, such rebel movements continued to draw followers until the middle of the 19th century, when Marxism, with its messianic flavour, became in a sense the new religion of those who were critical of the way in which society allocated its rewards.

Marx's answer to the inequities of a stratified social order was, of course, the creation of an unstratified one—the complete abolition of

continued on page 25

Garbed in Oriental-style costumes, six Hollywood starlets enjoy a game of mah-jong in 1922. So great was the demand for the sets of marked "tiles" used in playing the game that the Chinese ran out of the beef bones used to make them and meat packers in Chicago had to ship supplies of bones to China.

"Everybody's doing it"

Every once in a while someone starts spinning a hula hoop or playing an ancient Chinese game called mah-jong (*above*); suddenly, it seems everybody's doing it. A fad has been born.

Psychologists say fads grow—and die—out of concern for both status and conformity. In taking up a fad the individual usually is conforming to the behaviour of his peers or another person he admires. He gains prestige by being one of the first to master the fad and earns praise by showing off his skill in performing its techniques and his inventiveness in developing new ones.

In fact, sociologists say that to be successful a fad must afford broad possibilities for individual variation. "The hula hoop was an ideal fad subject because each child could develop his own particular variation in spinning the hoop," noted Ralph Turner of the University of California at Los Angeles. The more variations an individual develops, the more status he acquires. And when the possibilities for innovation are exhausted, the fad begins to lose its ability to confer status, and it dies.

Bed pushers from Ontario's McMaster University are halted momentarily by a blizzard while setting an endurance record—the team pushed a bed on bicycle wheels 510 kilometres in 43 hours. The fad of marathon bed pushing, born in Canada, spread to California, and enjoyed a brief, bone-wearying vogue in 1961.

Kimono and all, a Japanese woman spins a hula hoop. This craze began in the U.S. but spread to Europe and Japan, where 16,000 hoops were sold in a week.

Bursting out of a Volkswagen, 40 students at Long Beach State College claim a record for "cramming", a craze on American campuses during the 1950s.

A handy substitute for a fig leaf is hastily provided by a policeman rushing to cover up a streaker who delighted fans at a British rugby match in 1974.

private property and the establishment of a society in which the wealth would be evenly distributed. At the opposite pole of social and economic theory, 19th-century socialists, led by Herbert Spencer, who cited Charles Darwin's theory of evolution, had argued that the biologically qualified always rose to the top of the social ladder; he concluded that stratification was therefore not a human invention but rather a universal law of nature. Recent history has, if anything, tended to bolster this conservative opinion.

Moreover, many theorists who formerly advocated a restructuring of society now hesitate to place their faith in such a simple solution. Theologian Reinhold Niebuhr, who once argued cogently for a new society, eventually came to place the blame for social inequities not on the structure of society but on the character of man himself. An "entrenched predatory self-interest" existed in everyone, he said, whether he was "benevolent or not". The great delusion, said Niebuhr, lay in a simple-minded social radicalism that did not recognize how quickly "the poor, the weak, the despised of yesterday may, on gaining a social victory over their detractors, exhibit the same arrogance".

No doubt the prevailing ideas about the good or evil of social stratification will change again, just as they have done in the past. What is unlikely to change, however, is man's almost universal preoccupation with stratification itself, a social phenomenon that affects every facet of his existence and that he has at no time in his history been able to control or fully understand.

So basic is the impulse to stratify society in one way or another that among one group of people, the Betsileo of Madagascar, even the dead are stratified. The Betsileo believe that a dead man can either gain or lose status, depending on the magnitude of the postmortuary services he performs for the living in return for their offerings and prayers. A study that was conducted several years ago even suggested that status may extend far beyond the grave. A team of researchers who were looking into the backgrounds of saints in the Roman Catholic Church found that a person's chances of achieving sainthood were enhanced by advantageous birth: of the 2,494 people canonized between the First and 19th centuries, 78 per cent were upper class, 17 per cent middle class and only 5 per cent lower class.

Indeed, most sociologists maintain that only temporarily can any society remain unstratified. In a small group that formed accidentally —for example, by shipwreck—comparative strangers might suspend for a time their normal social distinctions. But eventually, even here, a leader of the group would emerge, and functions would be assigned or assumed, depending on the composition of the lifeboat community. A new ladder of status would be created. In fact, British playwright J. M. Barrie delighted and discomfited turn-of-the-century London audiences with just such a theme in his satire, *The Admirable Crichton*. In the play, a pompous English lord and his languid, haughty daughters are shipwrecked on an island along with several servants, including the versatile butler Crichton. That worthy's skill and resourcefulness make survival possible—he even creates electric lights, piped water and speaking tubes. Eventually Crichton emerges as the natural lord of the island and is served worshipfully by his former master and mistresses. (The point is not spoiled by Barrie's own snobbishness, which caused him, at the end of the play, to cast his vote for the British caste system. Rescued and back in England, all the play's characters revert to their former positions even though they recognize Crichton as the superior individual. The butler himself proclaims: "There must always be a master and servants . . . for it is natural.")

If society is indeed structured like a ladder, then the glue that holds the ladder together is conformity. If the system is to work properly, its members must accept certain kinds of behaviour as appropriate for each rung of the ladder. This appropriate behaviour may be directly related to the function that gives a person his status in the first place; obviously a physician is expected to be professionally competent. But other requirements for conformity may be irrelevant—a physician is likely to lose status, and perhaps even his practice, if he treats patients while he wears a bizarre costume. The pressure to conform to society's rules and regulations in fact begins at birth with the training of the infant and continues throughout the whole of an individual's life. It is the price society exacts for a desired status.

In order for people to conform to the requirements of society, sociologists say at least one of three elements must be present. On the one hand, an individual must feel that the act of conforming is pleasurable or that it offers a prospect that he can find enjoyment in. Or, as a second possibility, he must regard conformity as a moral duty of the individual. Or, finally, he must consider that conformity is necessary in order to obtain the acceptance and respect of other people. Whatever the reason for conformity, it is necessary. If the ladder is to remain intact, large numbers of people must behave in accordance with their statuses. They must do whatever they deem is expected of them.

However, no one obeys the prescriptions and proscriptions of his society all the time, and the degree of conformity seems to depend on the status of the individual. People of very low social rank have little to lose by disregarding standards of appropriate behaviour, and other people dismiss their deviance, if it presents no threat to society, simply because they are unimportant. But a person of high status also may refuse to conform, partly because of his own self-confidence. Having reached the upper echelons of society, he assumes that his judgment is better than that of other people; he therefore takes the prerogative of deciding for himself how he should behave. But there is also less pressure on the high-status person to conform. In an extreme example, the world's most expert surgeon would still be sought after for his professional expertise even if he insisted on operating in his underwear.

Conformity to a group standard also seems to depend upon the size of the group that sets the standard. This facet of behaviour has been demonstrated repeatedly by tests of an individual's willingness to disagree with opinions contrary to his own. Confronted by only a single divergent opinion, he is just as likely to put as much credence in his own belief as he would put in the other person's. When two people oppose him, however, his self-confidence begins to waver, and when he is faced by

Footsore and legs smeared with grime, three girls at a birthday party convey with posture and expression their discomfort at conforming to a status that is being forced on them by their parents—that of proper young ladies.

The quiet courage of these civil rights advocates, solemnly filing across hostile Alabama during a 1965 freedom march, helped persuade

Americans to reform their social system, eliminating political and economic obstacles that had kept blacks from improving their status.

the opposition of three or four, his tendency to conform to the majority increases sharply. The pressure to go along with others soon reaches a maximum, however, and thereafter does not change no matter how large the group grows. This conclusion is drawn from a series of experiments that were conducted by psychologist S. E. Asch in which a single person was successively confronted by an opposing majority of two, three, four, eight and, finally, 16 people. In his experiment Asch worked with over 100 subjects and discovered that the tendency to change to the opinion held by the majority increased with the size of the majority until it included four people, but he found that after that it did not matter how many were involved.

Two other elements that may play a role in conformity are the goals of the group and the degree of the individual's identification with them. Each member is more likely to go along with group actions, even when he does not wholeheartedly agree with them, if the group is organized to achieve an end that is compatible with his own ideals. Francis Ambriere, in his study of men in a German prisoner-of-war camp during the Second World War, discovered that the camp population was subdivided into a number of tightly knit groups, each of which had different goals. One group consisted of prisoners who were openly defiant in their captivity and refused to work; another focused all its energies on working on plans to escape; while the members of a third group devoted their efforts to making the best of their enforced stay by ingratiating themselves with their captors. The individual members of each group were extremely loyal and conformed to their group's objectives, partly no doubt because of the threatening situation they found themselves in.

But any sort of uncertainty—even uncertainty that is much less critical than this—tends to make conformity seem not just urgent, but attractive. In fact, studies have shown that conformity is not really the coercive force that people commonly assume it to be. Since so many social benefits accrue from it—companionship, a sense of belonging, a role, a sense of achievement—it has been found that most people will conform willingly, and in doing so they discover a sense of identity in belonging to the group.

Strict conformity is essential in an authoritarian society. How it is instilled in Soviet children by the educational methods employed in the schools was explained in *Two Worlds of Childhood* by psychologist Urie Bronfenbrenner of Cornell University. The Soviet child, Bronfenbrenner wrote, is pressed from a very early age to improve his status by fulfilling the expectations of a steadily widening circle of compatriots, that is, to behave in the ways they think he should. First there is his family, then, later, his class at school, the school itself, his military unit, the whole of the armed forces, and ultimately the nation. To illustrate this point Bronfenbrenner reported a classroom incident he witnessed. A little girl was reprimanded by the teacher for forgetting the words of a poem she was supposed to recite: "Larissa, you have disappointed your mother, you have disappointed your father, and above all, you have disappointed your comrades who are sitting here before you." The worst punishment that could be devised for the Soviet school child was a loss of face, which means a loss of status.

Such an emphasis on pleasing others may be anathema to passionate believers in individual freedom, but a certain degree of conformity is necessary in every society. Some cultures are relatively tolerant of deviations, permitting their members to drop out or challenge the justness of the ladder. And almost every society must reckon with those who would do away with the ladder or radically alter its structure. But if the society is to survive, most of its members must conform to their status on the ladder. The glue must hold.

Levels of Importance

2

Back in the 1930s, W. Lloyd Warner and a task force of social anthropologists spent five years on an analysis of status in the town of Newburyport, Massachusetts. Warner had recently completed a field investigation of Australian aborigines, and he wanted now to study the social order of a contemporary American community.

The town that Warner and his colleagues selected is located at the mouth of the Merrimack River, about 55 kilometres north of Boston. Founded in 1600, Newburyport originally centred around a bustling shipbuilding and sea trade. By the time Warner and his colleagues began their investigation, it had acquired a population of 17,000 and the maritime enterprises had given way to an industrial mixture typical of the northeastern United States: factories making shoes, silverware and electrical machinery; a complex of building trades; and railway shops.

Warner and his colleagues gave the community the pseudonym Yankee City and began interviews and first-hand observations to dissect its social structure. What they found beneath Yankee City's placid surface was a sharply stratified social system, consisting of six status layers, which Warner designated upper-upper, lower-upper, upper-middle, lower-middle, upper-lower and lower-lower. Each of these status groups had its own distinctive character. The top rung of the ladder was occupied largely by Old Yankee stock, descendants of the English settlers who had come to colonial America two centuries or more before. This upper-upper was tightly knit. Its members married later than others and counted more single and widowed people among their numbers. They were mostly professionals and executives, but their ranks included the highest percentage of employable people who held no jobs at all. They sent their children to private schools, seldom intermarried with other groups, and were regarded by others as people of "good breeding" who knew the "right" thing to do.

As Warner and his colleagues ranged down the ladder, the picture changed decisively. Ethnically, the levels became more mixed. The lower-upper level—just below the top—included a sprinkling of people of Irish descent, and at this level, professional and executives were mingled with a few owners of wholesale and retail businesses. The two levels at the bottom of the ladder were viewed by the community as a constellation of groups, each of which was identified by ethnic background: Irish, Poles, Russians, Greeks, French Canadians, Italians, Jews, Armenians and Negroes. Occupationally the people in these groups were mostly semi-skilled workers and were employed in the shoe and silverware factories, transportation and building trades, and the town's small clamming industry.

But Warner found that neither lineage nor occupation—alone or in combination—was sufficient to determine status. Not all Old Yankees were upper-upper, and while most doctors were highly regarded not all were. Almost every attribute of an individual figured in his status. Wealth was an important consideration. The value of the property owned by the lower-lower group was less than a seventh of that owned by the upper-uppers. The factor of seven also applied to differences in family income. Religion, too, was an attribute that distinguished one level from another—the Old Yankees favouring the Unitarian and Episcopal churches and most people at the bottom worshipping at Catholic, Methodist, Baptist or Presbyterian churches.

Even law enforcement was status-related, for position in society affected the way people behaved—and the way the police viewed their behaviour. An examination of Yankee City's police records showed that the upper-upper level accounted for only one half of 1 per cent of the arrests, while those of the lower-lower accounted for 65 per cent. Moreover, none of the arrests of members of the upper-upper group involved people under 20 years of age, but 30 per cent of all the lower-lowers arrested were juveniles. Boys and girls in the higher groups, the study concluded, "frequently commit the same acts but do not get on the police records". It explained this discrepancy "as a product of the amount of protection from outside interference the parents can give the members of their families".

The findings of the Yankee City study have been confirmed in subsequent studies by Warner and other social scientists. In modern societies, elaborately stratified status systems are omnipresent, although five status groups are more common than the six that Warner found in Yankee City, since the upper crust of Old Yankee is the kind of group that does not exist in most places.

The status systems arise in response to definite social needs. Society has a broad variety of tasks of varying degrees of sophistication that must be performed. It persuades people to perform these tasks through a system of offerings and rewards. Individuals offer certain qualities —family ties, experience, training and abilities. Societies evaluate these offerings and then reward them with varying amounts of wealth, power and prestige.

In most countries today, occupations (*pages 46-47*) are a good guide to a society's evaluations of its members. People who hold the most difficult and responsible jobs usually are rewarded with more wealth, power and prestige than others, which means that they achieve the highest status. The profession of medicine is a good example. Society has a crucial need for trained people who can look after the health and physical well-being of its members. But it takes a great deal of money and a long and grinding preparation to become a qualified physician. Most societies therefore reward doctors with a high degree of prestige and substantial wealth in order to encourage people to undertake the

Dressed in formal gowns and white tie and tails, English upper-class tots dance daintily at a garden party. Like these miniature lords and ladies, all children learn early the roles they must play to behave in keeping with their status and thus perpetuate their social class.

arduous training demanded of members of the medical profession.

The system of offerings and rewards does not always work ideally or even fairly, of course. The competence and the contributions of some individuals may not be commensurate with the status that society confers upon them. Some people may be barred from the status ladder or denied access to some of its rungs by arbitrary or irrelevant considerations, such as race or religion. The distribution of rewards may be inequitable. But if a complex society is to function and survive, some system of meting out wealth, power and prestige must be devised. And despite repeated attempts throughout history to discover a means of assuring everyone an equal share, up to now all societies have included some people who have acquired more wealth, power or prestige than others, so that a status ladder has emerged.

The qualities and qualifications by which society sorts out individuals and arranges them on status ladders fall into two cateogries, called ascribed and achieved by social scientists. Ascribed qualities are those with which the individual is born, such as family, race and ethnic background. Achieved qualifications are those that the individual acquires or develops in the course of a lifetime—special talent, education, knowledge and experience.

In some societies, the ascribed qualities are all-important. An individual's family, race or ethnic background may fix his status for life. Caste systems, for instance, are closed, hereditary social groupings in which the individual's status is determined at his birth by the standing of his family.

The classic example of a caste stratification developed in India. Nobody is sure how the system began there, but most scholars think it dates back at least to a series of migrations by the Aryans, a central Asiatic people who came into India through the Hindu Kush passes about 2000 B.C. The Aryans conquered the native Dravidian tribes, who were of darker complexion than themselves, and then, according to one theory, set up a complex social hierarchy with Aryan Hindu priests, or Brahmins, at the top as a means of preserving their racial purity. Since the early Sanskrit word for caste is *varna*, meaning "colour", the original impulse towards a caste system may have grown out of the Aryan desire to remain distinct from their darker-skinned subjects. In any event, in time a hierarchical caste system emerged that was probably the most intricate example of social stratification ever conceived; it made Hindu India into the most ritualistic and the most completely segregated culture the world has known.

The holy books of Hinduism record that the Aryans originally divided society into four principal castes and assigned specific occupations,

continued on page 40

The famous winged ornament, double-R trademark and traditionally shaped chrome of a Rolls-Royce proclaim the wealth and power of its occupants. While many once-prestigious cars have become too commonplace to denote high status, the Rolls retains its lofty position as a symbol of luxury and affluence.

Symbols of affluence

The mark of status may be as obvious as a monarch's jewelled crown or an admiral's braid-covered sleeve—or as subtle as the double R on a Rolls-Royce. Some status symbols are universal and enduring: precious gems, fine clothing and elegant houses, for example. Others are transitory in nature; at various times the sign of the upper class was a little black dress, a single strand of pearls, shoes by Gucci or luggage by Louis Vuitton. But the foibles of fashion are surpassed by the eccentricities of cultures, for status symbols have varied greatly from one society to another.

In Imperial China a man's affluence was attested to by his wife's feet—so deformed by bindings in childhood that she could not walk on them unaided, thus proving her husband could afford a wife who did not work in the shops or fields. In modern Venezuela, Alsatian dogs have been a status symbol, and in Western Europe many aristocrats flaunt rings with their family crests. The perfect status symbol, one sociologist concluded, is something that is not only readily identifiable and expensive, but difficult to obtain. A nice Rembrandt, say, or the Hope diamond.

*Chief of a nomadic Persian tribe, a
Bakhtiari man proudly shows off three of
his four wives and a few of his children.
A Bakhtiari's status is gauged by the
number of wives he can afford to support.*

An Afghan woman is practically hidden by three indications of her wealth—a brocade cape, a jewelled nose ornament and an armful of glittering bracelets.

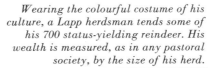

Wearing the colourful costume of his culture, a Lapp herdsman tends some of his 700 status-yielding reindeer. His wealth is measured, as in any pastoral society, by the size of his herd.

Garbed in a crazy quilt of opulent colours, a Nigerian nobleman sits astride an equally well-adorned horse. His turban, his many gowns layered one over another and the cloths that cover his saddle are all symbols of his noble status.

39

duties and privileges to each. The Brahmins at the top were priests and scholars; the Kshatriyas, administrators and warriors; the Vaishyas, merchants and farmers; and the Sudras, common peasants and labourers. Beneath these castes, and virtually outside the social order, were the Untouchables, who performed the most menial tasks that the Indian society had to offer. The castes were arranged on a graded scale of social prominence depending on their supposed derivations from the god Brahma's body—the Brahmins themselves having sprung from his mouth and the others in descending order having come from his arms, torso and feet. In actual fact, there were probably always more than four basic castes; in modern times there have been as many as several hundred.

The system that prevailed in India through the ages had deep moral and philosophical roots. The basic Hindu social assumption is that men are born unequal. Coupled with this idea is a belief in transmigration—that is, the belief that the soul will be reborn in an unending succession of worldly incarnations. The sum total of a man's thoughts and actions in his previous incarnation is known as his karma, and it is this karma that determines the position into which he is born. During his lifetime he has certain prescribed social and religious duties that he must carry out. Collectively, these duties are known as his caste rules of dharma, meaning "that which is right". Depending on how well he fulfils his dharma—that is, depending on what spiritual credits and debits he manages to accumulate—the individual can alter his karma so that he will rise or fall in the caste system in the next incarnation. But in his present incarnation he is completely powerless to move; indeed, his only possible path to salvation is to accept the position into which he was born as the expression of what he has earned on the wheel of life. Thus, whatever the origins of the Indian caste system may have been, its practical effect through history was to put a moral sanction on the inequality of fixed status: if a man was born an Untouchable it was because his past behaviour entitled him only to that status.

What made the Indian culture seem unfathomably complex to Western eyes is that the principal castes were subdivided into *jati*, or subcastes. Nobody knows just how many of these *jati* emerged, for subcastes were forever combining or dividing. They certainly numbered in the many thousands, however: government sources estimated that there were at least 2,000 subcastes among the Brahmins alone.

The subcaste was the basic unit of Hindu society, and it was with the subcaste rather than the caste itself that the individual's loyalties lay. It might be expected that all the members of subcastes of a single main caste would have a great deal in common. But most of the Brahmin subcastes spoke different tongues and could not understand one another. Taboos restricted relations between castes and subcastes alike. In theory, for instance, marriage between castes or subcastes was forbidden, and so was dining with members of another caste. And in southern India it was even believed that a member of a lower caste could pollute a Brahmin holy place simply by approaching it. In some places, a lower-caste shadow could pollute a higher-caste shadow just be crossing it, and the very sight of a lower-caste person could be polluting. The Untouchables are still widely thought to pollute the ground that they walk over and until only recently they were required to keep to special paths. In Kerala, the various subcastes once had to follow rigid rules that governed the number of paces they had to remain apart when passing one another in the street, and the Namboodiri Brahmins used to be preceded by runners shouting "Ha-ha!" as a warning to lower-caste persons to remain 60 paces away.

While the concept of pollution was of great importance to Hindu life, and was stressed in great detail in the early sacred texts such as the Laws of Manu, it had little to do with cleanliness itself. Devout Hindus might shrink from a bottle of boiled water that was presented to them by an Untouchable but at the same time they would freely drink tumblers of water from the holy Ganges River, even though the victims of infectious diseases and the half-charred bodies of those who were cremated on its banks were thrown into the waters.

Pollution and the purification rites necessary to avoid it largely accounted for the seemingly endless caste and subcaste duties that served to govern virtually every aspect of a Hindu's life cycle. It is difficult indeed for a Westerner to imagine the minutiae of daily living that were subject to prescribed ritual. The exact hours for bathing, the kind of receptacle from which water could be drunk, the way in which the hair or nails could be cut, the direction in which people were supposed to urinate, the proper time for sexual contacts, the kind of food to be eaten and the method of its preparation, the colour of the clothes or of the flowers to be worn, even the type of sweets allowed to be offered to ancestors —all these and myriad other details were prescribed. A child learned the rules and the intricacies of pollution very early in his life and, according to the English author G. M. Carstairs, had learned by the age of seven to reject food that was offered by an Untouchable with the words "I shall become touched". A Hindu could come no closer to another Hindu than the rules of pollution permitted.

No two subcastes did anything precisely the same way. The Chungia Chamars smoked their pipes differently than other Chamars, for example;

*A reverent Frenchman kisses the ring of Cardinal
Eugenio Pacelli—who later became Pope Pius XII
—in an act of homage to the prelate's high-ranking
office as a prince of the Roman Catholic Church.*

the Dobaile and the Ekbaile were both subcastes of the Telis, but the Dobaile yoked two bullocks to their castor oil presses and the Ekbaile only one. The very length of the twigs with which a man cleaned his teeth varied from subcaste to subcaste.

These differences may seem trifling to Westerners, but when multiplied to include every aspect of daily living, they created gulfs between one subcaste and another that eventually led to a highly fragmented society. One Indian author described a Brahmin girl of the Deshastha subcaste who took the most unusual step of marrying a Brahmin man of the Chitpavan subcaste and felt that, in doing so, she had entered an entirely new universe. She found, for instance, that she differed from her mother-in-law in every aspect of running the house; the two of them even prepared the same vegetables in different ways. The Hindus might be the majority in India, but each Hindu subcaste was a minority dwelling in its own special world.

The average Indian villager living in his subcaste was enclosed in a tradition that somehow held society together for millennia. It provided him reassurance and self-confidence for it offered certainties and structure in his life; he knew exactly where he stood and exactly how he should act. How well he adhered to the ritual dictates of the tradition would determine his status in the village. It was even highly likely that his occupation would be chosen for him—in Bihar he would be a leather-worker if he was of the Chamar caste, for example, and a fisherman if he was of the Kewat caste. He inherited the god he worshipped. Thus if he was a Maharasthrian Brahmin he worshipped Ganesh, the elephant-headed god, and if he was an Andhra Brahmin he worshipped Hanuman, the monkey god. He lived in a house that was surrounded by relatives and in a street that was largely filled with members of his own subcaste. Most of his social life revolved around the family, but if he were to venture into mixed-caste groups he would know precisely where he should stand or sit in relation to the others and in what sequence he and the others should be served food or drink. If it happened that he had to eat with people of lower castes, he was able to avoid pollution by sitting at a small table to one side, thus dining with the others and yet not dining with them simultaneously.

There were several other methods of bending the ritual rules to suit the occasion. An orthodox Brahmin, for instance, would without hesitation patronize an Untouchable prostitute, carefully performing a purification rite afterwards that in effect wiped out the contact with her. Similarly, although the hill Brahmins of Kumaon believed that they polluted themselves when they used the plough because it was a tool that was used by the Sudras, they nevertheless ploughed the land and pretended

they did not by erasing the act afterwards through purification. Nobody questioned these inconsistencies. They were, in fact, part of the very fabric of a uniquely elastic social system. The Indian writer Taya Zinkin illustrated this flexibility when she compared Jewish sanctions against the eating of pork with the Hindu prohibitions applying to beef. She recalled that when the first Israeli ambassador to Britain went to dine in Buckingham Palace, he would only eat hard-boiled eggs, oranges and bananas that he peeled himself, for fear of eating something that might possibly have come into contact with plates that had contained pork. By contrast, Zinkin told of a highly devout Brahmin woman who sent her son off to study in England and advised him to eat beef to help ward off the cold, damp climate, although she herself worshipped the cow as divine. "When you come back, I will have you ritually depolluted", the mother told him.

This elasticity in ritual helped prevent the caste system from strangling Hindu society. More important to essential flexibility, however, were basic limitations on the effect of caste. It might affect but did not necessarily fix an individual's wealth, power and prestige. First of all, there were poor and illiterate Brahmins and wealthy and educated Untouchables, and within every caste there was wide diversity of background and resources. Second, the direct correlation between caste and colour, while possibly a factor in ancient times, no longer existed in India in more recent times: most upper-caste members tended to be light-skinned, but there were black Brahmins and fair Untouchables, and their caste rankings were not altered by their complexions. Third, while occupations were roughly divided along caste lines, there were many exceptions: agriculture was open to any caste, the military recruited soldiers who were not Kshatriyas, and many castes had priests who were not Brahmins.

In addition, there always existed a certain degree of mobility in India, although it was largely a mobility of caste rather than of the individual—for instance, the members of an offshoot of a caste could perhaps move up a notch or two by changing their occupational roles and by following with special strictness the various ceremonial regulations having to do with prayers, fasting, cleanliness, reading of the sacred literature and so forth—although they could never move from one principal caste group to another one. In this fashion, certain segments of the Pasi caste gradually gave up hunting and fowling in order to become farmers and fruit-sellers, occupations that were more highly valued by the society. These Pasi caste members then constituted a new subcaste and they were therefore barred from marrying into the families of their old subcaste. This tendency of castes to split apart, with one

An occupational guide to status

Butcher, baker, candlestick maker . . . a man is known by what he does for a living. The best indicator of an individual's status is occupation, partly because income is tied to it, partly because some jobs require more knowledge or skill than others, and partly because society attaches more importance to the functions performed in some jobs than others. Yet the industrial world's occupations may be rated differently from culture to culture.

The charts below, which were drawn from studies made in the 1950s and 1960s, compare the rankings given various occupations by people in England and Wales, Japan, Sweden and the United States. Different lists were used

ENGLAND AND WALES

1. Physician
2. Company director
3. Lawyer
4. Accountant
5. Civil-service executive
6. Business manager
7. Factory manager
8. Clergyman
9. Farmer (owning more than 40 hectares)
10. Reporter
11. Elementary-school teacher
12. Building contractor
13. Travelling salesman
14. Policeman
15. Chef
16. Insurance agent
17. Newsagent and tobacconist
18. Clerk
19. Carpenter
20. Plumber

JAPAN

1. Professor
2. Physician
3. Executive
4. Mechanical engineer
5. Civil engineer
6. Elementary-school teacher
7. Buddhist priest
8. Policeman
9. Clerk
10. Railway-station employee
11. Farm owner
12. Shop owner
13. Carpenter
14. Barber
15. Taxi and lorry drivers
16. Printer
17. Sales clerk
18. Baker
19. Tenant Farmer
20. Coal miner

SWEDEN

1. Professor
2. Company director
3. Elementary- or secondary-school teacher
4. Ship owner
5. Chemist
6. Head cashier
7. Colonel in the armed forces
8. Shop owner
9. Captain in the Merchant Navy
10. Barber
11. Jeweller
12. Carpenter
13. Accountant
14. Typesetter
15. Taxicab owner
16. Policeman
17. Sales clerk
18. Non-commissioned officer in the armed forces
19. Building labourer
20. Travelling salesman

in preparing the four studies, but the results produced some striking resemblances. Professors came out on top in Japan and Sweden and tied for fifth in the United States (but were not included in England and Wales). Doctors ranked high in Japan and in England and Wales, but were not in the top 20 in Sweden, where, for a variety of reasons, doctors do not command as much respect as in other countries.

Only the top 20 rankings are listed here from the European and Japanese studies; all 46 are given for the United States. In some cases, a number of occupations tied for the same rating, although only a representative one may be included here.

UNITED STATES

1. Supreme Court justice
2. Physician
3. Nuclear physicist
4. Government scientist
   State governor
   Cabinet member
5. Professor
   Congressman
   Chemist
6. Lawyer
   Foreign Service officer
   Dentist
7. Architect
   Judge
   Psychologist
   Clergyman
8. Company director
   Mayor
   Department head in state government
9. Civil engineer
   Airline pilot
   Banker
10. Biologist
11. Sociologist
    Schoolteacher
12. Captain in regular army
13. Accountant
14. Factory owner
    Building contractor

- Artist
15. Musician
    Economist
16. International Trades Union official
    Railway engineer
17. Electrician
    County agricultural agent
    Printing-shop owner
18. Machinist
    Farm owner and operator
19. Undertaker
    Social worker
20. Newspaper columnist
21. Policeman
22. Newspaper reporter
    Radio announcer
23. Bookkeeper
    Tenant farmer
24. Insurance agent
25. Carpenter
    Manager of small shop
26. Local Trades Union official
    Postman
27. Railway conductor
    Travelling salesman
28. Plumber
29. Car mechanic

- Playground director
30. Barber
    Machinist
    Snack bar attendant
31. Corporal in army
32. Lorry driver
33. Fisherman who owns boat
    Retail clerk
34. Milkman
    Bus driver
    Lumberjack
35. Restaurant cook
36. Nightclub singer
37. Petrol-station attendant
    Dock worker
    Railway worker
38. Night watchman
    Coal miner
    Waiter
39. Taxi driver
    Farm labourer
40. Caretaker
    Bartender
41. Clothes presser
42. Milk bar attendant
43. Sharecropper
44. Sanitation worker
45. Street sweeper
46. Shoe shiner

part moving up in the society, accounts for the fact that for centuries the number of castes steadily increased.

In contemporary India, however, both legislation and the pressures of industrialization have tended to work against the continuation of the caste system. Untouchability was officially outlawed in 1955, and the government has reserved a certain number of jobs specifically for the 55 million Untouchables and has set up scholarships for their children. Untouchables have become legislators and even cabinet ministers, and the government has decreed that all village councils must include in their number at least one representative of the Untouchable caste. Intermarriage between castes is becoming increasingly common, and in offices, factories, trains and buses, people of different castes mingle in a way that never would have happened even a generation ago. Many social scientists, however, believe that caste is so tenaciously rooted in the Indian psyche that the present efforts to eliminate it, just like repeated attempts in the past, will eventually fail.

Segregation systems that resemble caste still prevail in other parts of the world. The *buraku-min* in Japan (*page 49*) are poverty-ridden pariahs who live in dilapidated slums. South Africa's rigid policy of apartheid, with its separate social ladders for white, coloured and black peoples, is a caste-like system. The black man in the United States was consigned to a caste-like status until recent years, living in slavery up to the time of his emancipation during the Civil War, and restricted to the bottom of the economic and social ladders for many years afterwards. Women in many societies have traditionally been accorded a caste-like status in which their roles as housekeepers and cooks were decided for them at birth.

Caste is perhaps the purest example of ascriptive status, the status an individual receives by being born into his particular family. Such qualifications—the inherited offerings in the offering-reward scheme of stratification—are important in most of the world. In the Soviet Union, being related to an official is of great value, as is clearly evidenced by the statistics on the family backgrounds of young people who win admittance to universities. No one in Britain doubts the head start on the status ladder that goes with noble ancestry, nor in the United States is there any question about the similar advantage that accrues to Old Yankee families (the elevated status of Boston Old Yankees is so reminiscent of Hindu caste that they are called Brahmins).

Ascriptive status has been steadily declining in significance everywhere in the world as achievement has come to count for more and more; today what an individual does is more important in determining his status than who he is. This change has led to the concept of class as a

A stone's throw from a modern block of flats in Kobe, a buraku-min child plays in front of the jumbled shantytown where he lives.

Buraku-min: the outcasts of Japan

In Japan there are three million people who look like their neighbours, speak the same language and eat the same kind of food, but are regarded as outcasts. Called the *buraku-min*, or hamlet people, they are identifiable only by their birthplaces or current addresses in 5,000 slums scattered over Japan.

Most *buraku-min* can get only menial jobs. But even those who are economically more successful are rejected socially; intermarriage with other Japanese is rare. Discrimination against *buraku-min* dates to the 16th century. Japanese society then was rigidly stratified, with the samurai, or warrior class, at the top and the ancestors of the *buraku-min*, the *eta*, or filthy ones, at the bottom.

The outcast system was outlawed in 1871, but isolation of the *buraku-min* persists. Even today, the stigma of being a *buraku-min* is so humiliating that outcasts going home by bus may get off a stop or two early rather than reveal their shantytown addresses.

guide to status. The terms upper class, middle class and lower class have been divided and re-divided—working class, leisure class, upper-middle class and so forth—to indicate various levels of modern stratification. To most people, class still includes connotations of ascriptive qualities; inclusion in the British upper class generally depends on birth into an upper-class family, or at least into a very wealthy one. To sociologists, wealth is the crucial element, and they use the term class to refer simply to an economic grouping, to encompass those people who are more or less in the same income bracket. Those who are in the upper class are wealthy, those in the lower class poor. In industrialized societies, the individual's economic standing is the best indicator of the value society places on his qualifications. Thus wealth is usually accompanied by both power and prestige.

For this reason, in most modern societies the surest and quickest guide to the status of an individual is his occupation, because the job that he holds often determines his economic standing, which, in turn, generally determines his power and prestige. This close relationship between occupation and status is especially valid in relatively new communities that have grown up around industries and do not include a hierarchy of first families who derive their status from their ancestors. The corporate status ladder usually corresponds closely to the status ladder of the community. The head of the corporation generally enjoys high status both on the job and in the community at large, and the other employees of the corporation derive their class and status principally from their jobs.

The modern awareness of class as an economic concept emerged from the theory that was enunciated by Karl Marx in *The Communist Manifesto* and *Capital*. For Marx, the single most important feature of classes was their economic self-interest. In every society, he argued, there emerges a dominant class that controls most of the resources of the society and a subordinate class that provides the services for the dominant class. Class conflict is inevitable, he maintained, for the privileged naturally want to retain their privileges, and the underprivileged want to take them away (*Chapter 5*).

One of the main criticisms levelled at Marx was that because he was born into the upper bourgeoisie he never really understood the working class. "For Marx," wrote Edmund Wilson, "the occupations and habits, the ambitions and desires of modern man, which he himself had never shared, tended to present themselves as purely class manifestations, the low proclivities of an ignoble bourgeoisie. He could not imagine that the proletariat would take to them." Marx was unable to foresee that great masses of workers might someday live contentedly in a capitalist

Lacing Miz Scarlett's corset in Gone With the Wind, actress Hattie McDaniel plays the maid to perfection. Menial roles were all this talented black actress ever was allowed to play—in 83 films she was always a cook or maid. Such stereotyping—in American films of the 1930s, almost all blacks were menials, and most Italians gangsters—reinforced popular misconceptions that certain groups could not rise above low status, and helped "keep them in their place".

state, sharing the affluence and adopting much of the life style of the bourgeoisie, yet this is precisely what has happened in the great industrial states of the non-Communist world. The affluence that followed the Second World War has led to an expansion of the middle class in France (*pages 60-71*), West Germany and Japan, and a corresponding shrinkage of the working class has occurred, thereby altering the social structure and also reducing class antagonisms.

But if things have not turned out exactly as Marx expected, his analysis of history and society and his understanding of the crucial role played by economic classes still remain a feat of the imagination. While class antagonisms have failed to materialize with the force that was predicted by Marx, economic class is one of the strongest social forces and one of the most powerful influences on behaviour. Sociologist Harold Hodges Jr. quoted an American example. "Evidence hints that the middle-class Negro is much more similar to the middle-class Caucasian than he is to the lower-class Negro", Hodges said. "His choice of clothes, his voting habits, his manners and mannerisms, will be more recognizably middle class than Negro."

The importance of class as a determinant of status and behaviour can be seen in Britain. Although its once-rigid class system has been greatly weakened since the Second World War by socialization and a general levelling of the quality of life, sharp contrasts in life styles still depend on economic class. The influence of class can be seen from a magazine report on Britain's economic situation that chose to take a close look at the everyday activities of two men, John Owen and Doug Peach, who represented the upper-middle and working classes. Both were employed by Britain's largest privately held company, a supplier of motor-car parts named Rubery Owen Holdings.

In 1975 John Owen was the company's managing director; Doug Peach was the union convenor, or chief spokesman, at Rubery Owen. As a member of the upper-middle class, Owen lived at a country estate that included some six hectares of land and a large house surrounded by groomed lawns, flower beds, a pond and a paddock for the family pony. In the mornings at 8.30 he packed his two daughters and young son into a red Jaguar sports car and dropped them off at their private schools before proceeding on his way to work. At Rubery Owen, he occupied a quiet, panelled suite, working there most of the day and emerging only to lunch with other officers of the company. In the evenings, he generally stayed at home and played bridge with his wife and a neighbouring couple.

Doug Peach lived in a two-bedroom terraced house in a village located nine kilometres from the plant. In the mornings, he visited his garden behind the house to look at the vegetables that he was cultivating there. At 7.30 he drove to work in his year-old Ford, settled down in his drab, ground-floor office, and complained as he tried to telephone the works manager, "Management is just getting out of bloody bed." He spent most of his days participating in union negotiations and labour disputes, went home when the four o'clock whistle blew, put on some worn suede slippers, fed the chickens and tended the garden before settling himself into a comfortable chair and dining on cheese and cold cuts while he and his wife watched television. In the evenings he might pay a visit to the small pub next door for a pint or two of beer, or join the local cribbage team for a match against another working men's club.

Owen was clearly upper-middle class, while Peach was just as clearly working class, and the distinction between the two men was mainly one of economics. Peach obviously could not afford a home like Owen's. But economics had nothing to do with such other marks of status as the fact that Owen played bridge with his wife and a neighbouring couple while Peach played cribbage with other workmen. Those differences in behaviour arose from the contrast in their family backgrounds and their education: Owen was the grandson of the company founder, and Peach was the son of a bricklayer.

Such nuances mean that, while economic class is a major determinant of status and of life styles, it does not completely explain social stratification. The positions of some members of society cannot be accounted for in economic terms. The priest is accorded high status in most societies, and yet he usually ranks low in terms of wealth. His status is a product of the prestige that is accorded his profession rather than a matter of economic class. Conversely, there are some men of great wealth whose social status is not commensurate with their economic standing. The clearest example of this is the don of an American Mafia "family"; he may be very rich but his status, in society at large, is the low one of a criminal.

The German sociologist Max Weber recognized this discrepancy in the 19th century. Weber, who was perhaps the most influential social theorist since Marx, spent much of his career challenging Marxian concepts. Arguing that Marx's identification of status with economic class was too limited, he suggested that social esteem, or prestige, and power

Status so affects behaviour that these relaxing Britons are readily classified by the caps they wear, the stout they drink, and the meeting place they have chosen—the Miners Welfare Institute. In England anyone would recognize them as members of the working class.

Proper protocol for servants and masters

There are not many places left in the world where servants are expected to know their place. But it is only a relatively brief time since the impassable distance between above stairs and below stairs was everywhere as obvious as in the picture on the right and in the master–staff relationship that is prescribed in the excerpts below, from *Vogue's Book of Etiquette* for 1948.

THE BUTLER'S MANNERS AT THE DOOR

A butler should open the front door briskly and alertly and with a hospitable manner. In other words, he should open the door wide, and step aside, so that the guests need not sidle by him. If the visitor has come for business reasons, the butler usually asks him to wait in the hall.

INTRODUCING NEW MEMBERS OF THE STAFF

When an employee has just entered the household, a quasi-introduction to members of the family is sometimes necessary. The following examples will give an idea of the very elastic form. To her husband, the mistress of the house says, "This is Norah, who just arrived today." The husband answers, "Oh, how do you do, Norah?" and the maid says, "Thank you, Sir," or, less formally, "How do you do, Sir?" To a grown child, the mistress of the house says, "This is Norah. I don't think you've been here since she came," and, turning to the maid, "Mrs. Pyne (or Miss Rosalie or Mr. George) is my daughter (or son), Norah." Children are introduced with a phrase such as, "Say 'How do you do, Norah?' Jimmy. He's a big boy for five years old, don't you think, Norah?" After such an introduction, it is not customary to shake hands.

WHAT TO AVOID

No guest or member of the family except a very small child should ever be introduced to the employee. "This is my husband,

The gulf between classes is evident as Hungarian diva Hannah Horty is served by a maid.

Norah," or "This is my daughter, Hardy," is impossibly wrong.

THE MANNERS OF A CHAUFFEUR

This is the formal little routine of manners for a chauffeur: He stands by the door of the car, holding it open, when anyone gets in. Unless he has been given orders by the passenger, he asks for orders as soon as the passenger is seated. When the order has been given, he touches his cap as he says, "Very good . . . ," again using the standard form of address. Then he closes the door and takes his place at the wheel. The perfectly trained chauffeur does this briskly and neatly, and always goes around to the door near the wheel; he does not slide across the front seat. If orders are given him while he is driving, he nods without turning his head and again says, "Very good . . .".

In cold weather, the chauffeur stands by the door holding the motor rug folded over his arm. (It should not, incidentally, be called "the robe".) When the passengers are seated, while he is being given his orders, he puts the rug over their knees. This used to be the footman's job, just as it used to be the footman's job to open and close the door; old-fashioned chauffeurs never left their place at the wheel. Now that footmen have almost entirely disappeared, the chauffeur has taken over. Other ways of handling the motor rug are these: it is folded in convenient vertical pleats, on the far side of the back seat, and when the passenger is seated, the chauffeur draws it across his knees; or it may be tucked along the motor-rug cord, so that the chauffeur can lift it back over the passenger's knees as soon as he is seated.

were also contributory factors in determining status.

Lloyd Warner confronted the same problem when he undertook his study of Yankee City. "It was believed that the fundamental structure of our society, that which ultimately controls and dominates the thinking and actions of our people, is economic," he said, "and that the most vital and far-reaching value systems which motivate Americans are to be ultimately traced to an economic order." But in the study Warner found that he encountered various discrepancies that he was unable to explain simply in terms of the economics involved. "Several men were doctors," he wrote, "and while some of them enjoyed the highest social status in the community, and were so evaluated in the interviews, others were ranked beneath them although some were often admitted to be better physicians. . . . A banker was never at the bottom of the society, and none in fact fell below the middle class, but he was not always at the top. Great wealth did not guarantee the highest social position. Something more was necessary."

Warner found that the criteria by which the people of Yankee City ranked a fellow citizen included his "education, occupation, wealth, income, family, intimate friends, clubs and fraternities, as well as his manners, speech, and general outward behaviour". He used the term social class to differentiate among the various groups in Yankee City. "Social class is not the same as economic class," he said, explaining that "by social class is meant two or more orders of people who are believed to be, and are accordingly ranked by the members of the community, in socially superior and inferior positions."

Warner's definition of social class, it seems clear, equates them to status groups. He was facing up to the need, which had been anticipated years earlier by Weber, to account for people whose status could not be explained in terms of wealth, while at the same time recognizing the importance of economic factors.

Warner emphasized the importance of behaviour as a determinant of social class. He quoted Yankee City residents who said that in order to achieve a high position it was essential to "do the right things", and others who said, "You have to have a little money, but it is the way one uses it which counts."

The Yankee City study showed that behaviour and social class go hand in hand. Demonstrations of that fact can be found almost anywhere in the world. In most countries, the upper classes have a sharply defined code of behaviour, and anyone who expects to be included in their privileged ranks must behave in the same manner as they do. Alan Ross of Birmingham University set forth some of the arcane principles of British upper class, or U, behaviour in his widely acclaimed

Indistinguishable in the cotton jacket-and-trousers costume worn during the Cultural Revolution by nearly all Chinese, young people on a train trip from Canton to Peking read together from the book Quotations from Chairman Mao Tse-tung, which proclaims the necessity to build a classless society.

U and Non-U essay, which was first published in 1956. "The games of real tennis and piquet, an aversion to high tea, having one's cards engraved (not printed), not playing tennis in braces, and, in some cases, a dislike of certain comparatively modern inventions such as the telephone, the cinema, and the wireless, are still perhaps marks of the upper class," Ross wrote, and he added, "Again, when drunk, gentlemen often become amorous or maudlin or vomit in public, but they never become truculent."

Less noticeable behaviour is also influenced by social class. According to sociologist Harold Hodges Jr., studies of stratified communities have shown that people at the same status levels were "often markedly alike (and markedly unlike those in adjacent levels) in realms so diverse as aspirations, neurotic symptoms, political values, infant-training and child-rearing practices, leisure time pursuits, moral and religious beliefs, manners of dressing, speaking, and decorating homes, consumption behaviour, and responsiveness to such mass media as magazines, newspapers and television".

Class membership also strongly affects society's attitude towards the individual throughout the entire course of his life. Studies have shown that even fashions in child-rearing practices follow social class lines. A middle-class mother is more likely to coddle her child than a lower-class mother. "Class differences in feeding, weaning, and toilet training show a clear and consistent trend," reported Cornell psychologist Urie Bronfenbrenner. "From about 1930 till the end of World War II, working-class mothers were uniformly more permissive than those of the middle class. They were more likely to breast feed, to follow a self-demand schedule, to wean the child later both from breast and bottle, and to begin and complete both bowel and bladder training at a later age. After World War II, however, there has been a definite reversal in direction; now it is the middle-class mother who is the more permissive in each of the above areas."

Other studies have shown that as a child grows up, social class influences his teacher's attitude towards him in school (she is likely to be more sympathetic towards him if he comes from a middle- or upper-class family than a lower-class one). After he is married, the chances that his marriage will last are also affected. A study of Americans by sociologist William Goode of Columbia University showed that the higher the occupation, income and education, the lower the divorce rate—"There was an inverse correlation between class position and divorce rate." But this result held true only among white Americans. Among non-whites, he noted, "the higher the education, the higher the proneness to divorce".

Similarly, satisfaction with a job increases with higher social class. "The essence of higher class position," explained sociologist Melvin L. Kohn, "is the expectation that one's decisions and actions can be consequential; the essence of lower class position is the belief that one is at the mercy of forces and people beyond one's control, often, beyond one's understanding."

In non-working hours, the amount of time that the individual spends watching television is also class related. A 1974 study of the subject showed that lower-class Americans spent more than 16 times as much time watching television as did those of the upper class. And when a person dies, his status follows him to the grave. For even the kind of funeral he is given, the quality of his coffin and the size of his tombstone may be determined by his status. In most Western countries the relationship is likely to be a reverse one: those of high status generally prefer simple funerals, while those of the lower classes often go to their resting places in lavish style.

Breaking into France's new elite

The Daniel Jouves of Paris (*right*) are living proof of the sociologists' axiom that the more industrialized a society becomes, the more rungs are added to its status ladder, and the easier they are to climb. The industrial expansion that followed the Second World War restructured society in France. The drive to modernize succeeded so well that by the 1970s the country was the fastest-growing industrial nation in Western Europe; the new prosperity created a need for engineers and executives and produced a burgeoning upper-middle class. Able and ambitious men who wanted to rise quickly were provided with glittering avenues to status and success.

One who made the ascent was Daniel Jouve. The son of a self-made lawyer, Daniel studied law at university, then spent two years at Paris' prestigious Institut des Sciences Politiques, one of the schools that train the elite in business and government. "I went there," he once said candidly, "because it was a means to step up in the world. Afterwards I got a scholarship to Harvard Business School, not because I thought the training would be more scientific than at some other American schools, but because it was the Number One."

From there Daniel joined an American bank's manager-training programme. But, he commented, "I felt condemned to 'being stuck'," so he joined a French publishing house. Within weeks he was president of the company, a post he held for several years. In 1974, he joined a new publishing firm, where he began a business magazine, *Le Nouvel Economiste*. The magazine prospered, elevating Daniel and his family to the life style of the upper bourgeoisie.

Daniel Jouve and his American-born wife, Alice—with children Patrick, six, Alexandre, three months, and Cristin, nine—gather in their six-room flat in a fashionable district of Paris. The flat was elegantly decorated by Alice Jouve.

PHOTOGRAPHED BY GILLES PERESS

With a French under-secretary of state, Jouve makes a point over a pre-luncheon drink. The official had been invited to discuss current events at one of the twice-monthly lunches Le Nouvel Economiste *gives to keep its employees informed.*

High rewards for hard work

Daniel Jouve's position as publisher of an important new magazine forced him to work so hard that his wife worried as to how long he could stand the pace. But Jouve said, "I would not do it if I didn't enjoy my work. Actually, I love what I do." His middle-class origins also made him appreciative of the rewards of the job, present and future. "We were seven children," he recalled, "and my parents were not rich. So I have no personal fortune and my work allows me to build an economic basis for my future. My final aim is politics, and I am now in a good position for creating contacts."

With his department heads, Jouve thrashes
out a problem presented at a weekly
meeting. Soft-spoken and slow in his
arguments, Jouve nevertheless reserves
for himself the responsibility for settling
all questions, no matter how minor.

With chiefs of multi-national corporations,
Jouve listens to the simultaneous
translation of a German speaker at an
economic seminar in Davos, Switzerland.

63

Jouve celebrates a high point in his career—the successful first six months of his magazine—at a lavish cocktail party at a Paris hotel. Le Nouvel Economiste's format, which is patterned on that of American news magazines, was largely conceived by Jouve. Happily for his career, the format worked: reception was so favourable that within weeks of the magazine's appearance on news-stands, its circulation had reached 120,000.

Wife, mother, author, cook

Like her husband, Alice Jouve was a well-educated product of the middle class. A Bostonian who studied at Paris' Sorbonne University on a scholarship, she was teaching French when she met Daniel, then at Harvard. Though she sacrificed some of her aspirations to his, both Jouves believe a wife should be more than the-woman-at-home.

To this end, Alice managed to write a college textbook on mediaeval Paris. Though it took her several years to complete in her free time, she nevertheless plans to work on another. And she took up teaching again, conducting a course in French for Americans.

Notre-Dame Cathedral forms the back-drop for an outing with the children. Though Alice Jouve has help with the housework, she prefers to look after the children's upbringing herself.

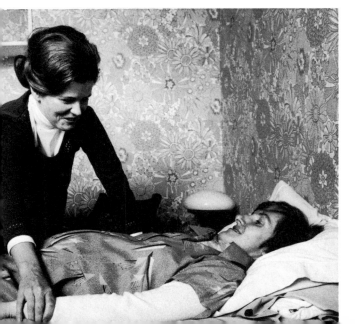

Alice Jouve sets the table for a festive dinner she prepared. "I do all the cooking and serving at our parties," she said, "the cooking because I see it as a creative art, and the serving because I think it adds a warm touch of hospitality that you don't get at maid-served dinners."

Assisting a friend with exercises for the painless childbirth method developed by Dr. Fernand Lamaze, Alice Jouve pursues a strong interest. "I'm a moderate feminist," she says, "and for me women's liberation begins with liberation from the fear of pain in childbirth, so that a woman can give birth with dignity and joy."

Romping with his son, Jouve convulses the boy by leaping awkwardly through fallen branches in a winter forest.

The prestige of a rural retreat

The importance in French society of a *résidence secondaire*, or country house, was analyzed in 1973 by American anthropologist Laurence Wylie. Wylie noted that though such dwellings used to be restricted to the rich, now many of the more prosperous middle class own them, while the upper classes retain their social superiority by seeking a third and even a fourth residence.

The Jouves are among those who recently acquired a country house, but it means more to them than just prestige. In the serene countryside, Daniel can spend time with his children, who see little of him when he is working.

Indulging in a country pastime that is fashionable among the French upper-middle class—but one that Alice Jouve enjoys for its own sake—she prepares for a gallop on a horse from a local stable.

Ending a long working day as he often does, with a social evening that is still tied to business, Daniel Jouve joins Alice in entertaining a magazine employee and his wife in Paris' smart Lasserre restaurant. Jouve's successful climb up the business ladder made him cheerfully philosophical about the fact that his work was never-ending. "After all," he smiled, "an interesting part-time job does not exist. Therefore, I really have no choice."

Going Up-and Down

3

The oldest tales of human drama, predating even the Bible, centre upon the rise and fall of an individual's fame and fortune. Such stories provide a gallery of unforgettable characters. There are the rogues who clamber to the top, regardless of cost to friends and loved ones, such as Sammy Glick in *What Makes Sammy Run* or the callous lover Joe Lampton in *Room at the Top*. There are the flawed, tragic figures like the brazenly opportunistic Julien Sorel in Stendhal's *The Red and the Black* who climb to the top only to fall to the bottom again. Then there are the God-fearing, hard-working heroes in Horatio Alger's sagas of poor boys who make good, and the fairy-tale heroines like Cinderella and Snow White who progress from hovels to palaces. And in the real world, history books and newspapers document the rise of political leaders like Fidel Castro and Nikita Khrushchev (*left*) or captains of great wealth such as the Rothschilds, Rockefellers and Onassises.

These real-life and fictional protagonists experience on a grand scale the sufferings or joys that come to millions of lives as status changes through social mobility. To social scientists, social mobility can be either "horizontal" or "vertical". Horizontal mobility involves a sideways movement from one region or country to another, or from one organization to another, with no change in status.

Of far more interest in the study of human behaviour, however, is vertical mobility—the movement of individuals up and down the ladder of social stratification. It is vertical mobility that gives most societies their restless natures, as people from the lower rungs of society move into the middle classes or into the elite, and members of the upper crust decline in power, wealth and prestige. In some highly dynamic, or open, societies, this circulation of people on the status ladder is rapid and involves large groups. In relatively closed societies such as India, vertical mobility is more limited.

Despite a popular belief that vertical mobility is a modern phenomenon of the industrial age, the fact is that most societies throughout history have offered ways for talented and ambitious individuals to rise to the top. The Old Testament relates how Joseph's gift of interpreting dreams elevated him from Egyptian slave to chief counsellor of the Pharaohs. Similarly, David's prowess with sling and lyre aided his rise from shepherd to King of Israel. In the Roman Empire, one historian noted, at least 36 recorded emperors made their way to the top from the lower strata of society, as did 12 of the 65 emperors of Byzantium and 55 of 144 popes on whom genealogical data is available.

Even during the mediaeval era, peasant boys became monks and acquired learning that led to eminence, or became soldiers and acquired booty and followers that led to power. The pace of mobility accelerated as modern times opened. There is a detailed 200-year history, beginning in the 16th century, of a bourgeois French family named Barbou who rose step by step through the ranks of a society dominated by landed aristocracy. The first Barbou of note owned a small printing establishment in Lyons. The Barbous moved from there to Limoges and eventually to Paris, all the time expanding their business bit by bit. Meanwhile, they accelerated the family's upward movement by paying increasingly large dowries for advantageous marriages of their daughters to husbands of higher social class. At the beginning of the 17th century, a Barbou daughter had a dowry of 1,000 livres; 50 years later, it was four times as much; a century later it had gone up another nine times. By then, the Barbous had improved their business position by acquiring a monopoly on printing the classical texts for all the Jesuit colleges in the province of Guyenne. With the fortune this coup brought them, they acquired first the fief of Couriers and then the seigneury of Monimes and other estates.

None of these aristocratic properties conferred nobility, but they made a marriage into the nobility possible and even probable. Pierre Barbou, *marchand à Limoges*, adapted his printer's colophon as his arms and registered the family arms in the *Armorial Général*. In 1748 the noble connection finally arrived, in the form of marriage between Pierre Barbou's daughter and Count Melchior de Carbonméres, at a cost to the family of 36,000 livres. In 1784, Pierre Barbou paid a large sum to the crown to acquire an office conferring permanent hereditary nobility on the family. The Barbous put a *de* and a family property after their name; the long upward climb was ended. Working as a family, they had moved in two centuries from the modest middle class to the nobility by following a classic formula: success in business, favourable marriages, buying of landed properties and the purchase of a title. Ironically for the Barbous, their triumph was followed in five years by the French Revolution, which toppled the aristocratic regime and made the holders of titles outcasts and fugitives.

The meteoric rise of gifted individuals or the gradual ascent of families like the Barbous remained fairly isolated occurrences before the 19th century. The advent of the Industrial Revolution, however, introduced horizontal and vertical mobility of a new magnitude, revolutionizing opportunities for status change and advancement. Between 1870 and 1950 in the United States, for example, the number of farm workers declined from half to less than one-eighth of the working population, most of the ex-farmers shifting into industries. So, too, did most of the arriving immigrants, who numbered about a million a year until 1925. Similar patterns of shifts from farm to factory work took place in the industrializing countries of Europe.

The factories, growing markets and proliferating technology opened many new job categories for technical and administrative specialists that enabled members of the working class or their children to rise into middle-class occupations. A survey of 90,000 white-collar workers in Germany in the 1920s revealed that almost a quarter were the sons of the working class. And it appeared to the investigators that the rate of mobility was accelerating—while only 19 per cent of employees over 30 came from working-class backgrounds, 32 per cent of the younger employees did. Another study of mobility in Great Britain in 1912 showed that two-thirds of the owners, directors and managers in the cotton industry had begun their careers either as manual workers or in minor clerical positions. The ablest of the young earners "attend in the evening at technical classes," the authors of the study noted. "Of the best students, an appreciable number rise to positions as managers or independent employers in industry." As the Industrial Revolution progressed, upward mobility seemed to become almost the norm. In the United States alone, more than 4.6 million men moved into higher status jobs between 1920 and 1950.

Social scientists now reckon the magnitude of the movement by the number of children who achieve a higher status level than their parents. The most important movement is from blue collar to white collar, the transition from manual worker to office worker, from using skilled hands to using a trained brain. This occupational shift is the one sociologists count in gauging mobility. By this criterion, the present rate of mobility in the most open societies of Europe and North America is about 30 per cent—about three out of every 10 sons and daughters are able to acquire higher status than their parents. The highest rates of mobility are found in the United States, Germany, Sweden, Japan, France, Switzerland and England.

The promise of a meteoric rise was held out to poor boys by cheap paperback novels, popular in the early 1900s. In their plots, a lowly errand boy or newspaper seller won the chance to make his fortune as a result of a heroic act, like leading fellow workers to safety in a fire (above).

In some countries, much upward movement results from a comparatively recent but determined effort to promote advancement among the lower classes. For example, the British government has, since the Second World War, encouraged and financed higher education for the children of the lower classes. As a result, some 30 per cent of the students in English universities are the sons and daughters of working-class families. In addition, graduates of the state-supported secondary schools now dominate top positions in government—a stark contrast to the days when the Empire was ruled almost exclusively by the products of illustrious privately financed schools such as Eton and Harrow. And numbered among the leaders of British industry recently were the sons of a gasworks mechanic, a tailor, a baker and a travelling salesman. In France, on the other hand, the top jobs still tend to go to a rather narrowly based elite drawn from a dozen or so prestigious colleges known as the *Grandes Ecoles.*

A 30 per cent rate of mobility leads to highly dynamic societies, with nearly a third of each generation occupying a different social position than their parents. At the same time, that estimate means the majority of people follow their parents' status. Some people do not need to strive upwards: they are pushed. This has been the case in countries with succeeding waves of immigration. In the United States, for example, millions of European immigrants who came to the country beginning in the 1880s spoke no English and entered the job market at the lowest level, thus pushing native-born workers one or two notches up the occupational ladder. Mexican and other Latin American workers who arrived later then filled the bottom slots, pushing the European-born immigrants up the ladder. And still later, American blacks and Puerto Ricans made their bid for occupational advancement and were, in turn, consigned initially to the lowest-level jobs.

The pace of mobility clearly depends on the times. There is much upwards movement during periods of expansion, such as the entire world saw during the Roman era and the West experienced over the past five centuries. In static societies movement slows, and in years of economic contraction it reverses. Yet the times only affect opportunities. It is the individual who directs his shifts in status. He must, consciously or unconsciously, make a personal decision to undertake the often arduous trek towards the top. Usually, his decision will require a period of special training in preparation for a particular rung on the ladder. And generally he must expose himself to greater risks than those experienced by people who are content to remain at the same occupational level as their parents. A number of studies have attempted to isolate the characteristics separating such persons from their peers because it is from

The reality behind the myth of the poor boy who rises to fame and glory was lived by youngsters like these. Hawking papers in the streets of New York City around 1900, they worked long hours in all kinds of weather for pennies. And although a few ex-newsboys—Dwight Eisenhower, Bob Hope—became famous, most never got very far above their lowly start.

the ranks of the ambitious that society fills its most important technical, professional and supervisory positions, all the way from the shop fore-man who directs the work of skilled labourers to the leaders of government, business, science and art.

Obviously, upwardly mobile persons must be highly motivated. And in the view of most social scientists, this motivation is provided chiefly within the family. It is no surprise that upper-class families with a record of achievement pass along to their children the drive for achievement. A study of Nobel Prize winners in the sciences from 1901 to 1950 revealed that "the fathers almost always are of very high social position: nobility, upper-rank officers, upper-class businessmen, lawyers, ministers of religion, etc." In England, a handful of outstanding families has handed on a tradition of achievement through successive generations from the early 19th century to the present. In families such as the Macaulays, Stephens, Darwins, Arnolds, Huxleys and

Churchills, each new member has been inspired to pursue an individual course up the ladder of success. Such motivation has helped some members of these families overcome what might have been crippling handicaps. Virginia Woolf, born a Stephen, and Aldous Huxley both achieved literary greatness, although Woolf suffered severe depressive illnesses and Huxley was a victim of recurrent eye trouble.

While much of the will to strive upward may be traced to the family background, such motivation does not appear to be equally distributed among offspring. In a survey that traced the links between birth order and personal achievement, American psychologist William D. Altus found that in both England and the United States, first-born sons and daughters were more successful than their younger siblings. Altus' survey, which drew upon studies going back to 1874, also determined that the eldest child was more likely to achieve higher status if his siblings were brothers, rather than sisters, and that the ablest and most likely to succeed of all may be the only child. In attempting to explain the greater potential of the first-born child, Altus and other researchers suggested, among other things, the likelihood that such children imitate adult behaviour more than younger children, and also may be more curious. Some researchers proposed that first-born children usually receive more disciplined supervision than the relaxed upbringing accorded younger children. Such discipline, it is reasoned, may benefit the elder child in his efforts to succeed.

The role of the family, however, can also be a powerful restraint upon natural talent, ambition and mobility—a handicapping influence that keeps many people from ever embarking on an ascent up the ladder. In one study of family influence upon the individual, sociologist Joseph A. Kahl selected from working-class families in the Boston area 24 boys who had demonstrated sufficient intelligence to go on to college. All of them had done well in their early school years, but by the time they reached high school—for reasons they themselves did not completely understand—most were not performing as well as middle-class boys whom they had easily surpassed previously.

Kahl gently probed for the explanation in their family backgrounds. With considerable sensitivity, he interviewed each of the parents at length, and from their comments he etched some touching portraits of people who were convinced that their children were locked into fixed positions in society. These parents believed it would be futile for the child to struggle to improve status. "I tried to tell him he isn't going to be a doctor or lawyer or anything like that. I told him he should learn English and learn to meet people. Then he could go out and sell something worthwhile," one father, a bread salesman, told Kahl. "I suppose

Following father's footsteps

In the dozen years after the Second World War, a number of surveys measured occupational mobility in industrial societies. As the chart below shows, the surveys in three representative countries found that such mobility was high, as a substantial minority of sons moved out of their fathers' job categories. In the U.S. the minority swelled to a majority among small farmers, forced to leave the land by automated agriculture.

Predictably, the least movement was among those already at the top—office workers and professionals—while the upward mobility of the sons of skilled and semi-skilled workers remained consistently high in all three countries.

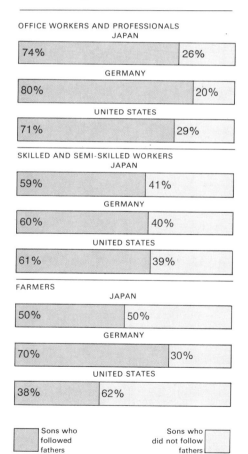

OFFICE WORKERS AND PROFESSIONALS
JAPAN

| 74% | 26% |

GERMANY

| 80% | 20% |

UNITED STATES

| 71% | 29% |

SKILLED AND SEMI-SKILLED WORKERS
JAPAN

| 59% | 41% |

GERMANY

| 60% | 40% |

UNITED STATES

| 61% | 39% |

FARMERS
JAPAN

| 50% | 50% |

GERMANY

| 70% | 30% |

UNITED STATES

| 38% | 62% |

Sons who followed fathers   Sons who did not follow fathers

there are some kids who set their mind to some goal and plug at it, but the majority of kids I have talked to take what comes, just get along." Other parents felt unable to help their children progress. A mother working in a chain store remarked, "I don't go to see the teachers. When I go up there I can't talk good enough. Some women go up there and, I don't know, they're so la-di-da. But I can't talk that way. Me, I'm just plain words of one syllable and that's all." This woman concluded, "I figure he'll get his knocks later on, and he should do what he wants to now. I don't make them do homework or anything".

These youths were endowed at birth with ample gifts for getting ahead, but the family influence rapidly put the brakes on their ambition. Neither the influence of teachers nor the example of schoolmates could do much to instil motivation in a child who was surrounded at home by negative attitudes towards achievement.

For all the influence of social class and family upbringing on an individual's drive for status, the advantages or disadvantages of birth are not decisive. The example of individuals who break out of the milieu into which they were born and try for something better—or at least something different—indicates something else at work. One such individual is Vehbi Koc, at one time described as the richest man in Turkey.

Born into the Ottoman Empire in 1900, Koc was the son of a literary scholar who, like most traditional Turks, scorned the pursuit of business and wealth. Such demeaning activity was left to the minorities like the Greeks, Armenians and Jews. As a young man, Koc recalled in an interview, "I noticed the minorities led a better life. Their standard of living was much higher than the Turks, so I decided to go into business". Koc weathered his father's disapproval and even talked the old man into lending him the equivalent of five pounds for business capital. With this, he plunged into the ranks of the low-status minorities and opened a small general store. When his home town of Ankara was made capital of the country in 1923, Koc began dealing in building materials during a construction boom. Five years later, he started selling Fords —then added a marketing outlet for an oil company. He negotiated joint ventures with foreign industrial corporations, culminating in his construction of a plant to manufacture the country's first home-built automobiles. Koc eventually came to control three score companies, and the wealth he built from his five pound investment became so great that he paid more than a million pounds a year in personal income taxes. His country's major philanthropist, he built hospitals and schools and financed hundreds of scholarships.

Attempting to isolate the quality that separates men like Koc—or, indeed, any person who strives to move up the social ladder—from his peers, psychologists have suggested the presence of a specific attribute, which they call the need-achievement factor. Individuals possessing this quality, it is believed, derive their primary rewards from accomplishing complex tasks. Motivated by a compulsion to achieve, they improve their economic and social position as a matter of course—almost as a by-product of their continuing drive to accomplish their objectives. A surgeon, for example, may be obsessed with the development of new and more effective operating techniques, which incidentally attract many patients, make him wealthy and also bring him the admiration and esteem of his peers.

Harvard University psychologist David McClelland made a study of this need for achievement in male university students. Comparing the results of dozens of tests and surveys that contrasted groups with high and low achievement scores, McClelland found that American males with a high need for achievement displayed such characteristics as a better memory for incompleted tasks, a willingness to volunteer as subjects for psychological experiments, greater involvement in college and community activities, a preference for experts over friends as working partners, and a greater resistance to social pressure.

McClelland's study confirmed the importance of family background as a motivational factor. Most of the people with a need for achievement, he observed, came from families in which the parents—especially the mother—fostered an early sense of independence, while at the same time providing warmth and encouragement as the child tried new things. McClelland's research also provided new support for the bold idea advanced over half a century ago by Max Weber, the pioneer German sociologist, linking achievement in modern industrial societies to the Protestant Reformation.

Weber theorized that Protestant ideology, beginning in the 16th century, created a new personality type dedicated to achievement. He argued that Protestantism produced such individuals because the religion placed a heavy emphasis upon a man's "calling"—a belief that he must do everything in his power to fulfil the station in life assigned to him by God. In addition, the early Protestant creed stated that certain people, the elect, had already been chosen and were predestined for heaven. In daily life, this meant that the only way an individual could reassure himself that he was one of the elect was to behave in every way as if it were a fact and to insist on success in everything he attempted. Finally, Protestant asceticism forbade spending wealth on luxury and comfort: the Protestant business man and entrepreneur, unable to spend his profits upon himself, had no recourse but to re-invest them in his enterprises, thus assuring that they would prosper even more.

Such a man, Weber stated, "gets nothing out of his wealth for himself, except the irrational sense of having done his job well".

McClelland expanded upon this religious basis for the drive to achieve by theorizing that it exists in every culture with an ideology that places the individual in a close personal relationship with his deity. Calling this relationship positive mysticism, McClelland maintained it instils a great need for achievement by requiring individuals constantly to prove their worth to their god. Thus, he argued, the Jewish religion contributes to a strong desire to achieve because it stresses daily self-reliance in living up to God's commandments.

Men and women who strive upwards on the social ladder undoubtedly are set apart by a stronger desire to achieve, whether it is a personality characteristic or a value instilled by family or ideology. But how they

A royal accolade marks the status of the Beatles as the rock singers are presented to Princess Margaret at a command performance in London in 1963. Show business has always provided a quick route up the class ladder. The Beatles rocketed from poverty in lower-class Liverpool to fame and fortune, becoming millionaires and cult heroes, admired and imitated worldwide.

go about it depends on time, place and personal inclination. The classic tale of social ascension is associated with a Unitarian pastor named Horatio Alger, who abandoned the ministry in 1864 to write the first of more than 100 books for boys extolling virtue and hard work as a formula for the rise from poverty to riches. In fact, most of Alger's heroes, small-town boys who have come to the city to make good, owe their success not so much to their own efforts as to the chance intervention of some benefactor. Typically, the hero renders the benefactor an unexpected service—rescuing his little daughter from drowning or from runaway horses. In return, the hero is taken off the streets and into the benefactor's business, where he is put on the ladder that leads to the board room. But success is also contingent upon the hero's moral credentials. "Have you any taste for liquor?" benefactor says to beneficiary in one typical exchange.

"'No, sir,' announced Hector promptly.

"'Even if you had, do you think you would have self-control enough to avoid entering saloons and gratifying your tastes?'

"'Yes, sir.'

"'That's well. Do you play pool?'"

Satisfied that the hero has no vices, the benefactor then gives him the opportunity that paves the way to success. In real life, social mobility depends, as Alger intimated but did not say, on luck. But advancement hinges, perhaps more than anything else, upon the individual's choice of the right channel upwards.

In a pioneering study of mobility published in 1927, sociologist Pitirim A. Sorokin outlined the traditional channels of vertical mobility: the military, the church, politics, professional and economic organizations, and education. The art of upward mobility depends upon an individual's perceiving which of these channels is the most fortuitous as times and circumstances change. The Roman Catholic Church, for example, has generally been a good route to improved status because it always has to recruit new members from the outside. In the past it was a far better route to social superiority than it is today, partly because it provided the only way a poor boy could get a good education but mainly because it ranked just after the aristocracy as the most prestigious calling. In modern times, however, the Church has lost much of its influence, and neither cardinals nor parish priests enjoy as much prestige or wield as much power as they once did.

A military career, on the other hand, can lead to astounding success provided that the soldier is able to find the natural outlet for his talents: war. It is unlikely that either Dwight D. Eisenhower or Charles de Gaulle —exceptionally able men—would have achieved their paramount

continued on page 87

Comedienne Fanny Brice (front, second from left) and song writer Cole Porter (rear, second from left) relax on the Lido in 1926.

High life on the Lido

The socially mobile of every era are sustained in their arduous climb by visions of themselves at the top, living it up among the fun-loving rich. Back in the 1920s, the visions were likely to centre around the Lido, or beach, at Venice.

The Lido first became fashionable in the late 19th century, when the new rage was sea bathing; swimmers flocked to enjoy the fine sandy beach facing the Adriatic's then sparkling waters. By the '20s, Venice's famous sea-front hotel, the Excelsior, was the place to go for European nobility as well as titans of commerce, industry and show business (*above*). The hotel spared no expense to keep its 500 guests amused: in 1925 it hired 300 actors, 100 soldiers and 30 dancers to act out the fall of Troy at one of its bi-weekly costume balls, with real horses and real flames.

By day, guests hung their cabanas with Oriental rugs in competitions for best-decorated beach tent. By night, they went to parties at private palazzos where the entertainment might include a Russian ballet corps. The more energetic raced around on treasure hunts, seeking such baubles as silver cigarette cases stuffed with lire. But most often they danced: fox-trotting, shimmying and Charlestoning around the clock, not only on land, but also on, and even in, water (*following pages*).

*Two-stepping under the Excelsior Hotel's
pseudo-Moorish facade—a decor that
was the height of elegance in the 1920s
—international playboys and flappers
dance across the floodlit, outdoor terrace.*

Rhythms of an amphibious band inspire a swimmer to high-kicking gyrations in the shallow water extending along the Lido.

Even the narrow confines of a floating cocktail lounge fail to quench this couple's enthusiasm for dancing as they gingerly execute a waterborne waltz to the strains of a boatful of musicians.

With luggage and liveried attendant in the tonneau, taxi-borne holiday makers take the ferry to Venice as they leave behind the posh pleasures of the Lido.

positions without the chance to show their worth in times of conflict.

The political channel of mobility tends to be chancy in democratic societies, but it is one of the most secure routes to higher status in socialist states. There, party loyalty and hard work can assure an ambitious individual many gains because the party pervades every aspect of the society and controls virtually all its positions of authority, including those in the arts, science and commerce.

Perhaps the riskiest of channels are wealth-making organizations—for example, the stock market—which by their very nature gyrate with the variable economy. Conversely, professional organizations such as medical societies, which enhance the prestige of an individual, are likely to be a sure route to higher status.

One route for advancement that Sorokin inexplicably omitted is provided by sex. The art of love and its practical pay-off—marriage—have long proved useful tools of advancement, as the Barbou family of France so clearly demonstrated. The Empress Theodora, who with her husband Justinian ruled over most of the civilized world from Constantinople in the sixth century, began as the daughter of a bear keeper. She took to the stage, where her lascivious performances scandalized chroniclers of the day. But she managed to snare the Emperor's heart, and he passed special laws enabling her to marry him and to become the most powerful woman in the world. Sex, however, is not solely a female stratagem. Ambitious young Russians during the reign of Catherine the Great found that the path to honours and wealth often lay through that lady's boudoir: one of her many lovers became King of Poland, another the richest man in Russia, while others picked up ambassadorships, military commands and princely titles.

Although advantages gained through sex and marriage continue to help many people climb in society, the principal route upwards in recent times has been the last on Sorokin's list: education. This method of improving status has an older lineage than most people realize. In ancient China, it was the only way. The durable Empire with its succession of dynasties was run by an educational elite, the mandarins. These scholar-bureaucrats earned admittance to schools and proved their capacity to rule by passing examinations. In the Chinese tradition, only the most capable pupils could gain the greatest status: neither humble origin nor exalted family station influenced test results.

But it was not until the Industrial Revolution that education became almost everywhere the key to mobility. The complexities of technological societies create an insatiable demand for trained people—for one thing, everyone must be able to read, write and calculate, a requirement that vastly expands the need for professional teachers. With so many opportunities, almost anyone who prepares himself to take advantage of them can do so. One of the most dramatic examples of the uplifting effect of education was provided when, after the Second World War, the United States government began underwriting university education for over 10 million demobilized soldiers. This injection of advanced training boosted so many of this group from lower levels to higher ones that, according to one estimate, the government gained an extra one thousand million dollars annually in income taxes (in return for a total expenditure on such education of $19 thousand million).

In Japan, schools at the primary and secondary level have assumed such importance in determining an individual's future that his chances of acquiring higher status are virtually decided before he is barely out of his teens. Schooling is critical because social advancement for most Japanese means joining the ranks of white-collar workers in one of the country's giant corporations. Once a person gets such a job—known in Japan as becoming a "salary man"—he can generally count on remaining with the company for life. During his career, promotions come regularly: he can usually predict when he will become, for example, the head of a department or assistant to a manager. Except during periods of unusual economic turmoil, employees are seldom discharged or made redundant, and the corporations provide far greater benefits—insurance, medical care, loans and housing—than are available to Japanese who are not salary men.

To obtain a corporate job that will set him up for life, however, the aspirant must be a graduate of one of the better universities. Getting the diploma at the end of his schooling is rarely a problem; Japanese universities seldom dismiss anyone, even for poor performance. The difficult stage in the individual's career is passing the examinations that will gain him admission to one of the better secondary schools, and then passing the examinations that qualify him for the limited positions open in the universities.

Competition in the examinations is so fierce that there has been a phenomenal growth in after-hours and weekend schools designed to augment regular school studies. Some 600,000 of these supplemental schools, called *juku*, are now in operation, attended by an estimated six million of Japan's 10 million primary-school children. The role of the *juku* is to provide extra instruction that will help children qualify for secondary schools, but the system has got so out of hand that there are now *juku* designed solely to help children get into the better *juku*. In practice, the *juku* system requires many Japanese children, nine to 12 years old, to study 14 or more hours a day, and in the more authoritarian schools they are punished when they make a mistake or nod over their books. The psychological toll of such early status competition is marked by an alarming number of suicides among children who despair over their academic prospects.

The view that advanced education is a guarantee of gains in income, power and prestige has been accepted for generations almost everywhere. In America it has led to bitter controversy, firstly because certain groups felt they were being denied access to education that might improve their lot, secondly because a respected Harvard University sociologist, Christopher Jencks, challenged the very idea that schooling contributed greatly to the economic gains of upward mobility.

During the 1960s, the conviction grew among many Americans that equalized education would overcome the disadvantages of poverty and deprived family backgrounds, and enable minority and lower-class students to improve their economic prospects. In the effort to redress inequalities in the educational system, various social programmes were launched, including pre-school instruction for culturally deprived children in the three- to five-year age range, massive public investment in educational facilities, and transporting—busing—children between poor and wealthy school districts, a measure that led to riots by enraged parents in many parts of the country.

In 1972, however, Jencks undertook a survey of how schools actually paid off in terms of one significant component of status—adult income. In a summary of the results of the survey, he noted: "In general, the pay-off from schooling is no better than the pay-off from going to work and putting your money in a savings account." According to Jencks, the data revealed that in many occupations, there was a barely measurable difference between the ultimate earnings of people who went to good or poor schools. Similarly, the amount of time spent in schooling also made little difference—except in occupations that demanded extensive academic credentials, such as medicine or engineering. For most members of society—railway engineers, factory workers, car dealers, grocers—Jencks concluded that the ultimate level of achievement could not be traced to any particular aspect of educational, family or class background. For example, brothers who shared the same family background and went to the same schools varied almost as much in their adult economic status as did any two persons selected at random from the population. To some observers, Jencks' finding—that the source of monied status cannot be traced to any pattern of family background, quality of school, or even intelligence—suggested the real answer may simply be the old Horatio Alger solution, pluck and luck.

If the ways to climb the social ladder seem ill-defined and change-

*The invitation above admitted the bearer
to a Cinderella story come true, the
1956 marriage of an American, Grace
Kelly, to one of Europe's few remaining
monarchs, Prince Rainier of Monaco
(left). Though she had been a movie star,
the bride's new status as a princess
represented a fantastic leap in rank; her
grandfather had been a poor Irish
immigrant, her father a bricklayer who
became a rich contractor but never
won acceptance in aristocratic society.*

able, the barriers to mobility are often brutally evident and highly resistant to change. Monied status is no guarantee of social acceptance, as many a climber—both fictional and real—has learned to his bitter regret. Such was the discovery of F. Scott Fitzgerald's title character in *The Great Gatsby*. For Jay Gatsby, the ultimate goal was Daisy Buchanan—beautiful, wealthy, from an old family, who gleamed "like silver, safe and proud above the hot struggles of the poor". Gatsby first wooed and won Daisy, despite his own impoverished background, as a soldier bound for war—disguised, in effect, as a "gentleman" by his officer's uniform. Upon his return, unable to cloak his low status in a uniform, he set about making a fortune. But his acquisition of wealth and a sumptuous house still did not qualify him for Daisy's love, for his economic success came from bootlegging and other disreputable pursuits. Gatsby suffered and ultimately died for Daisy, while she remained with her upper-class husband, who fitted just as naturally into the world of high society as she did.

Fitzgerald's tale illustrates the slipperiness of the topmost rung of the status ladder. Conscientious strivers can garner great wealth, public honours and all the material accoutrements of status, yet find themselves excluded from the zealously guarded preserves of the socially elite. In this heady world, the *haut monde* maintain their preserve by inventing and changing subtle, often unspoken rules of chic conduct. The parvenu then must demonstrate social worth by acting as though he also knew the rules. *The New York Times'* Charlotte Curtis observed the game at work while on assignment in the mansion-infested Florida wintering spot of America's "old rich", Palm Beach. Here, as one pillar of established society airily put it, "there are only 150 people worth knowing". Those who are worth knowing live by an arcane code of behaviour. Language and dress are carefully prescribed: "The boarding school accent used to be in. Now it's out," said one woman. "We wouldn't be caught dead in Puccis," said another, scorning the dresses of the Italian couturier. Renovating and decorating the elegant mansions is a fashionable pastime, more chic if the reason for the reconstruction is absurd. "I had the tile floor put in because the dogs like to lie on something cool," a Palm Beach resident explained. And fatuity seems to be a mark of acceptance. Curtis heard a woman remark, "I'm sure I'd feel wonderful all the time if I gave up eating. Food is bad for one".

Far more pervasive and pernicious than social snobbery are the patterns of ethnic and racial discrimination that close channels of mobility to millions. Prospects are considered poor for Catalans and Basques in Spain; Corsicans, Bretons and Alsatians in France; Walloons in Belgium; and Croats and Serbs in Yugoslavia. Most of these groups are

Super gifts for the super rich

"The very rich are different from you and me," said Scott Fitzgerald. "Yes," replied Ernest Hemingway, "they have more money." They also have ways to spend it that would not occur to ordinary people: the rich often lavish money on baubles that confirm their status.

For the super rich the ideal bauble is not only costly but imaginative. Perhaps the best guides to super gifts for the super rich are the Christmas gift catalogues of two legendary stores in Texas—Neiman-Marcus in Dallas and Sakowitz in Houston. One year they offered such trinkets as a private island and a bath full of diamonds, with catalogue prices starting at well over $2,000 or £1,000.

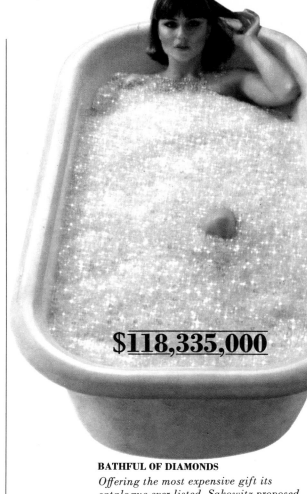

$118,335,000

BATHFUL OF DIAMONDS

Offering the most expensive gift its catalogue ever listed, Sakowitz proposed to cover an adult female to the neck in diamonds. The bath came free of charge.

$3,450

ANTARCTIC ICE BUCKET

The nickel-plated penguin cooler on the left, which sold for $450, became an even more unusual present when it was loaded with Neiman-Marcus' surprise extra— ice cubes chipped to order from a frozen chunk imported from Antarctica.

$8,650

PRO TENNIS LESSONS

Tennis is the game the Beautiful People play, and Sakowitz offered a day of tennis lessons with the noted pro John Newcombe at his camp near San Antonio, Texas.

$2,250,000

ISLAND IN THE CARIBBEAN

This 25 hectare island, an hour's boat ride south of Miami, could be charged to a Sakowitz customer's account. It came with master's and servants' lodgings, dock, boathouse and helicopter pad.

$2,600

MOONWALK TOY

This outdoor toy has a special bottom designed to give a child the "bounce of a trampoline, the fluid movement of a waterbed, the weightless sensation of a swimming pool, the fun of a carnival".

$3,640

HIS OR HER HOVERBUG

For mobile status-seekers, Neiman-Marcus suggested this two-passenger craft, which scoots over land, water, ice and snow at 70 kph, gliding on an air bubble.

considered peripheral by the national government, and opportunities for advancement through the traditional channels such as political organizations, corporations, the military or other routes are limited.

In many other nations, however, ethnic barriers have proved most restrictive for blacks. Sociologists Otis Duncan and Peter Blau concluded in their studies of the American job structure in the 1960s that blacks were the only group that could not rely upon performance as a means of getting ahead. Blau and Duncan cited as one gauge of this failure the fact that blacks at every level of educational achievement ranked far behind whites in the status level of the jobs they ultimately held. As a result, many talented and ambitious black Americans were forced to seek channels outside the mainstream of the economic and social structure, such as athletics or the performing arts. And even in these areas there were barriers: until recent decades black jazz musicians could not play their own music side by side with white performers, and it was only in 1955 that a black singer, Marian Anderson, first appeared with New York's Metropolitan Opera—upon the insistence of its Austrian-born general manager. More recently, opportunities for other black Americans have been gradually improving as they acquire more education, but black people generally still encounter many barriers to their advancement.

Women are another group restricted in opportunities for status. Until the past few decades, ambitious women depended on their husbands' achievements to carry them up the status ladder. Housewifery, teaching and nursing were the only acceptable occupations for a female—and still are in many countries. Even with the liberalization of social rules regarding the access of women to education, and to professional and business life, women lag far behind most men in terms of job prestige and pay. Part of the reason may be that centuries of subordination to men has instilled in women what Matina Horner, the psychologist who has served as president of Radcliffe College, called a fear of success. To demonstrate her thesis, Horner gave male and female undergraduates tests requiring them to write stories based on a given cue. One test contained as a cue the statement: "After first-term finals, John finds himself at the top of his medical school class". The stories written from this cue by male undergraduates were generally positive. One said: "John is a conscientious young man who worked hard. He is pleased with himself. John has always wanted to go into medicine. John continues working hard and eventually graduates at the top of his class".

However, when a similar test was given to women students and the cue placed a female, Anne, in the achieving role, typical results included such negative stories as: "Anne will deliberately lower her academic standing the next term, while she does all she subtly can to help Carl. His grades come up and Anne soon drops out of medical school. They marry and he goes on in school while she raises their family". Another wrote: "Aggressive, unmarried, wearing Oxford shoes and hair pulled back in a bun, [Anne] wears glasses and is terribly bright".

Summarizing the test, Horner reported that fewer than 10 per cent of the men responded negatively to a story cue about a successful performance, while 65 per cent of the women were disconcerted, troubled or confused by the cue. "Unusual excellence in women," Horner said, "was clearly associated for them with the loss of femininity, social rejection, personal or societal destruction, or some combination of the above." The most striking discovery was that most of these anxiety-ridden responses were from girls who possessed high intelligence and who came from achievement-oriented family backgrounds.

"Despite the fact that we have a culture and an educational system that ostensibly encourage and prepare men and women identically for careers," Horner found, "the data indicate that social and even more importantly, internal psychological barriers rooted in this image really limit the opportunities to men, especially in the post-adolescent years."

Another barrier to status gains—affecting both men and women alike—is fluctuating economic conditions. People may acquire all the requisites for an improvement in their status, then find that there is no place for them at the level they are fitted to occupy. In the most disruptive instances, youngsters are encouraged, even urged, to spend years of effort in training for a prestigious occupation, then denied the opportunity to make use of their talents by abrupt economic shifts. This was the fate of large numbers of young professionals in the United States during the late 1960s and early 1970s.

In 1957, after the Soviet Union launched the first space satellite, the American public erupted in competitive furore. Politicians declared that the schools had failed to keep up with the need for trained manpower. And so thousands of young men and women were urged to devote their careers to teaching and to science; millions of dollars were spent improving educational facilities and providing scholarships. The public mood was so science-orientated that in one opinion survey, nuclear physicists were found to rank just below Supreme Court justices in prestige. By the late 1960s, however, the campaign had proved too successful. Schools were graduating more scientists and engineers than the economy could absorb, and subsequent cut-backs in government support for research and for military and space hardware restricted the job market even further. By the early 1970s, both new graduates and many trained professionals found that their hard-won degrees and experience had set them up for no higher status position than a spot on the unemployment line. Young schoolteachers were especially hard hit by the combination of a declining birth rate and reductions in government spending, which caused educational jobs to contract. In the mid-1970s, applications for teaching jobs exceeded the number of openings by 97 per cent.

For many of these unfortunates, mobility was not up but down. Downward mobility, of course, is an inevitable consequence of social stratification. It has often been said, for example, that no family survives at the top of the ladder for more than a few generations. "Shirt sleeves to shirt sleeves in three generations" was the way the rags-to-riches tycoon Andrew Carnegie is reported to have put it. Such ups and downs have been documented in most societies. Pontus Fahlbeck published a statistical survey of the Swedish nobility in 1903, and reported

that between the 13th and 19th centuries, a third of all noble lineages in Sweden survived only one generation, and few lasted beyond four.

Many social tumbles were caused by apocalyptic events, such as the devastation of war or stock-market crashes. But there have also been individuals with a gift for making the least of their advantages, just as successful upward strivers make the most of their opportunities. One natural loser was Ireland's premier peer, Edward FitzGerald, the seventh Duke of Leinster. Born into a world of mansions, champagne and caviar before the turn of the century, FitzGerald was a high-living young rake who never expected to inherit the dukedom because an elder brother was still living. To settle his gambling debts, he entered into a bizarre arrangement with a moneylender in 1919: FitzGerald agreed to sign over his claim to all proceeds from his birthright in exchange for £1,000 a year for the rest of his life.

It did not seem a bad deal at the time, but two years later the unexpected happened. His elder brother died, and FitzGerald inherited estates and interests that should have yielded him a magnificent life style on an income of nearly £1,000 a week. But the improvident new Duke was bound to his bargain. For the rest of his life, FitzGerald's minuscule allowance from the arrangement declined in value and he went bankrupt four times—once even going to jail for obtaining credit illegally. At the age of 83, the Duke, who was truly to the manor born, died in a shabby two-room apartment paid for with an overdraft on his wife's bank account—"distraught, depressed and utterly penniless," his wife sadly noted. Like many others who have suffered such reversals, FitzGerald failed to grasp early on that there are social, legal and economic conditions even for the highest and seemingly most impregnable positions.

A more celebrated failure to understand the foundations of her status led to the downfall of the legendary Lady Hamilton, who was the mistress of England's greatest naval hero, Lord Nelson. After the deaths of her lover and also of her noble husband, Lady Hamilton's position in the highest echelons of early 19th-century British society depended only upon her inherited wealth, which she proceeded to squander. With the loss of her ties to status, she was quickly shunned by society. Ultimately she endured the disgrace of debtor's prison and died an impoverished exile in Calais.

Most people are willing to risk the fates of the Duke of Leinster and Lady Hamilton for the opportunity to rise to high status. Yet increasingly, social scientists are questioning whether society and individuals benefit—or suffer—from mobility. In theory, it breaks down class barriers, makes society more uniform and dissipates class prejudices and

Vestiges of status lost surround Hussain Ali Khan, 74, in this home in Lucknow, India—a single room with objets d'art that once adorned his family's palaces. Khan, ex-ruler of three states, lived in luxury on nearly £800,000 a year until the government seized his land in 1947, cutting his annual income to £1,600.

conflicts. On the other hand, some sociologists have argued that pre-occupation with mobility reinforces the class system: the individual who wants to rise out of the working class and into the middle class is not only accepting but also emphasizing the importance of class distinctions. Sociologist Gösta Carlsson, who conducted a notable study of mobility in Sweden, went even further. "Though the high rate of mobility may have the effect of diminishing some of the gaps between classes," he wrote, "it may also tend to conserve the system and ultimately even create inequality."

British sociologist Michael Young arrived at the same conclusion, by a different route, in a fable about a future English society that permitted untrammelled social mobility. In Young's imagined system, inherited position was proscribed; each person won his place in society strictly through merit—a combination of intelligence and effort. As a result, the elite was composed solely of the brightest members of society and the lowest classes of the dullest. But this ostensibly fair system had unwanted side effects. Previously, talent had been distributed through-out society and each class and group had its own natural leaders. Under the new system, the superior people were all truly superior, and the lower lower classes suffered the psychological and social stigma of being veri-fiably inferior. The social upshot was a ruthless and rigid class division and—as Young's satire would have it—bitter class resentments that led to violent reaction by the lower orders.

The social and psychological wounds of mobility in real societies have been examined by another sociologist, Melvin Tumin, in an article titled, "Some Unapplauded Consequences of Social Mobility in a Mass Society". In Tumin's view, society suffers when individuals who are rapidly moving up the ladder become too preoccupied with status. An obvious example is the politician who, elected as legislator, neglects the affairs of his constituents because he is too busy pursuing higher office. Another consequence, according to Tumin, is that in a highly status-conscious society, individuals tend to devote less energy and value to their work and productivity and place too much emphasis upon the trappings and badges of status. The result is a decline in the quality and the dignity of work. Individuals in such societies also are prey to personal insecurity when their worth is measured in terms of such status attributes as wealth. "In a society with differentiated income classes," Tumin wrote, "almost everyone is outranked by someone else who, by his own criteria, is more worthy."

Perhaps the greatest psychological toll is inflicted upon those who aspire to the heights, but fail to make the grade. Such, indeed, was the moral of Gustave Flaubert's novel about an ambitious woman, *Madame*

A family's rise and fall

The rise and fall of the Rudenschöld family (*below*) illustrates the slipperiness of the status ladder. The progenitor was a 17th-century farmer in Sweden. As the family climbed the ladder, its members included a bishop, a nobleman and a member of parliament.

This upward mobility was marked by name changes: a last name (from the native village) Latinized with "ius", as was temporarily fashionable, and eventually ennobled with "schöld" (shield) to indicate the right to bear arms. Family status started slipping after that, to primary-school teacher, then stationmaster and immigrant clerk in America.

THORSTEN
Farmer in Rudstorp

HAKAN RUDENIUS
DIED 1697
Clergyman; curate in Fryksande

THORSTEN RUDEN
1661-1729
Bishop of Linköping; poet

CARL RUDENSCHOLD
1698-1783
Ennobled 1719; made baron in 1749 and count in 1779; cabinet member

TURE GABRIEL RUDENSCHOLD
1759-1839
Army lieutenant colonel; member of Riksdag

THORSTEN RUDENSCHOLD
1798-1859
Army captain; administrator; primary-school teacher in Vastergotland

JOHANNES GABRIEL RUDENSCHOLD
1840-1879
Stationmaster in Engatorp

AXEL CASMIR RUDENSCHOLD
1875-1910
Clerk in Philadelphia

Bovary. The daughter of a French farmer, romantic Emma Bovary married a physician and might have settled down to a comfortable, provincial existence. But a chance invitation to a ball at the home of a noble—one of her husband's grateful patients—opened a new world. Reality was overwhelmed by fantasies of gilt ballrooms, haughty duchesses and brilliant chatter in society salons. In Emma's mind, "Theirs was a higher life, 'twixt heaven and earth, amid the storm clouds, touched with the sublime. The rest of the world came nowhere, had no proper status, no real existence." She took a series of fashionable lovers, borrowed deeply to dress herself and to buy them gifts, and finally bankrupted her long-suffering husband, plunging the family into ruin. Flaubert dispatched his yearning, flawed heroine according to the conventions of a good moral tale: she died a horrible death by poison, only slightly the wiser.

To a lesser but more realistic degree, Emma's crushed hopes are experienced by many who lose out in the rush for the rewards at the top of the social ladder—whether they are unsuccessful artists, corporate businessmen who fail to rise above middle management, or frustrated assembly-line workers who would be union stewards. The competition for progressively fewer places on the upper rungs of the ladder ensures success for a few and disappointment for many. Such concerns, however, are probably irrelevant as long as societies offer rewards to people for what they achieve. For people will go on striving as long as society, in Daniel Patrick Moynihan's words, continues to insist, "What you do is what you are: to do nothing is to be nothing; to do little is to be little. The equations are implacable and blunt, and ruthlessly public".

The making of a professor

Most families that ascend the social scale proceed by slow stages rather than spectacular leaps. Yet even when progress is gradual, the heights won by successive generations may lie beyond the imaginings of their forebears—simply because the means of advancement were unavailable in an earlier day.

Unforeseeable opportunities played a key role in the four-generational family saga traced on these pages. The story line leads from simple folk in the English countryside—a cowman and a woodcutter among them—to David Martin, a leading sociologist in London. Along the way, successive generations showed consistent energy and enterprise in responding to a series of larger social trends. A first crucial step by the family was to join the tide of population-movement towards cities, where opportunity abounded. One forebear became an engineer, another a chauffeur and taxi driver. David Martin, in turn, benefited mightily from a means of advancement that had been out of reach of his antecedents—education. His paternal grandmother was an illiterate who signed her children's birth certificates by marking an X; his mother received only a modicum of schooling; yet David Martin, making the most of the educational opportunities offered to his generation, has become a professor and a distinguished author in his field.

George Davey, the grandfather of David Martin's mother, was a woodcutter in Exmoor, in the west of England. He and his wife Ann had this studio photograph taken in 1880 in the local market town.

WALTER MUDFORD, FORE STREET,
ARTIST & PHOTOGRAPHER, TIVERTON

David Martin's grandfather, also George Davey, moved from Exmoor to the port of Weymouth, where he became an engineer in the waterworks. On this page of the family Bible, he appears with his wife Rhoda and one of his six children.

David Martin's paternal grandfather, Alfred Martin, was a cowman on a gentleman's estate at Ware, a village 50 kilometres north of London. Here, he shows off a prize bull.

City dwellers of thrift and industry

David Martin's father, Frederick Martin, left school at 12 to work as a groom at the big house of the district. He was hardworking, ambitious and thrifty (at the age of 15 he was paying four shillings and sixpence into a savings account each quarter). Moreover, he possessed a keen eye for opportunity. Just when motor cars were beginning to oust horse transport, he moved to London and became a chauffeur. His reliability and efficiency quickly found recognition: his employers included an archbishop, the Chancellor of the Exchequer and Prime Minister Herbert Asquith himself.

In chapel one Sunday, he met Miriam Davey, who had come to London from Weymouth to work as a housemaid. They married in 1928 and put down a deposit of £80—Fred's savings of 20 years—to buy a small semi-detached house in the respectable suburb of Mortlake. In 1929, Miriam's first child, David, was born into this frugal but independent household.

Still a country boy in 1904, 13-year-old groom Fred Martin holds two of his charges in the stable yard of the local squire's house at Ware, the Hertfordshire village where he was born.

In his London chauffeur's uniform (above) Fred—now 29—stands proudly by an employer's Daimler. His enterprising switch from horses to motors secured him a small but steady wage in the city.

Miriam Davey (right) was in domestic service when she met and married Fred Martin. Like him, she left school early, but her great respect for education was later an important stimulus to her son.

10, Downing Street, Whitehall, S.W.

Mr Frederick Martin was employed by Mr Asquith last autumn for about three months as a temporary chauffeur. Mr Asquith believes him to be a perfectly ho[...]

Fred Martin made a success of his job as a chauffeur. A letter of recommendation from Number 10 Downing Street, where he briefly worked for the Prime Minister, praises him for being "honest, trustworthy and sober".

A childhood of quiet security

Home life for David and his sister Audrey (six years younger) held no luxuries, but no real hardships either. At first, holidays were spent with the grandparents in Weymouth, whose serious and loving influence strengthened Miriam's encouragement of her children's academic and artistic abilities. Her hardworking husband Fred consolidated the family's modest independence; he paid off the mortgage, then bought a little car to go camping. When war broke out in 1939, he became a reserve policeman, which meant a little more money. Soon afterwards, he changed from chauffeur to cab-driver, bringing home £18 a week—more than six times his previous earnings. Eventually he bought his own cab, and worked as his own master until he retired at the age of 75.

A photograph taken in 1938 shows nine-year-old David at his first school—the Mortlake Church Primary School.

David, his father, and his sister Audrey set up camp in Scotland during the family's first holiday on their own.

Miriam's father, here in Freemason's dress, was an active community member and influential in David's childhood.

Buying his own taxi was Fred Martin's reward for a lifetime of thrift and industry.

In 1933, David and his mother stand beside the front gate of the trim house in suburban Mortlake where he spent his childhood years.

Up the ladder of learning

Fred's and Miriam's untutored abilities had brought them from rural and small-town circumstances to a self-respecting life in London. For their son David, education proved the door to further advancement. Naturally gifted, and conditioned by his parents' ethic of hard work, David profited by the widening educational opportunities of the period. He won a scholarship to a state grammar school and trained as a primary school teacher. But in 1956, sociology caught his interest, and after three years of teaching by day and studying by night, he took a first-class external degree in the subject at London University. Thereafter, successes came rapidly: in 1961 he became a lecturer at Britain's foremost social science school, the London School of Economics; in 1964 he was awarded his doctorate of philosophy.

In this photograph of the student body of Westminster College—one of Britain's oldest teacher-training institutions—David Martin sits fourth from the right, in the first row. He completed the two-year training course there with the aid of government grants totalling £96.

A snapshot taken in 1947 (left) shows David at 18 with classmates from Richmond and East Sheen Grammar School. For a working-class boy, a sixth form education was an achievement.

On the left, David Martin (back row, right) assembles with fellow staff members of a primary school in a slum area of West London, where he taught backward ten-year-olds from 1952 to 1955.

In a formal portrait to mark the award of his postgraduate degree in 1964, David Martin, grandson of an illiterate farmhand, wears the academic robes of a Doctor of Philosophy of London University.

The top of the tree

David's academic success was crowned in 1971 by promotion to full professor and head of the sociology department of the London School of Economics. At last he had the time to write books on the numerous subjects that preoccupied him professionally. The position also allowed him opportunities to pursue other longstanding interests, such as journalism and music, hitherto sacrificed to the need for constant work. And it led to contact with prominent world figures. In 1967, for example, he made a BBC broadcast on the subject of the monarchy—and then received the accolade of a personal invitation to lunch with the Queen.

During a sociology conference sponsored by the Vatican, David Martin attended an informal meeting with the Pope—and satisfied youthful journalistic ambitions by reporting the conference for a paper.

ROME CALLS IN SOCIOLOGISTS

David Martin reports

One of the most important developments of the ta... period is

questions ever to face the Church.

It began with a meeting of some 3,000 people in the Gregorian University to hear a discussion between Jean Daniel-... Harvey Cox and the ...hovec ...gue, in

A seating plan from Buckingham Palace (right) is David Martin's memento of a luncheon with the Queen. Below, a newspaper cutting reports the occasion and pictures the professor in his study.

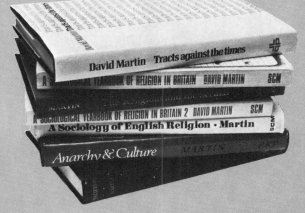

BUCKINGHAM PALACE

Luncheon Sitting List

TUESDAY

21st May 1974

Sir Oliver Millar

Mr. André Previn

Mr. David Carter   Mr. Colin Peterson

THE DUKE OF EDINBURGH   His Honour Judge Ruttle

Sister Mary Genevieve   THE QUEEN

Mr. Victor Page   Sir Peter Kent

                                    Professor David Martin

Sir Edward Ford

↑ ENTRANCE ↑

...to.
...t will also
...ublic toilets
...i-storey car
...he car park
...o the relief
...tion to the
... car park
...0 cars.
...ll. Another
... available in
...ar park pro-
... new Co-op.
...0 sq. ft. is
...w stores to
... the main
...thers are a
... for British
...d a 50,000

Prof. Martin is not sure why he was chosen but thinks it may have something to do with a recent broadcast of his on Radio 3 about the monarchy.

The broadcast on the programme "Personal View," followed the Princess Anne kidnap attempt in The Mall.

Whatever the reason, Prof. Martin found himself sitting down in the Royal residence to a lunch of melon, lamb, strawberries and cream, cheese and fruit.

... me
...Rome.
Prof. Ma...
mary scho...
ing at ...
class degr...
sity.
He is ...
demic, ...
ter. He ...
pianist ...
Method...
Road, ...
He ...
children ...
(11). I...

RES

D THEA-
...y 27th until
...enix Opera
...a Vie rari-
... Offenbach:
...ay 2.30 and

...until June
...by Patrick
...Vivien Mer-
... and David
...5 matinee
...day 5 and

...EATRE,
...g May 29th.
..." William
...g until
...ght Director
...ght director
...teers") —
...y, Wednes-
...enings 7.30
...ay 2.30 and
...2.30.

...evening in
... Group of

...rd to July
...the Moon"
...erformances
... and Thurs-
...iday 8 p.m.
...p.m.

...EATRE,
...- Starting
...ggerty," by
...week only).

...until June
...Rogers and
...ned by The
...e Society,
...Searing.

Professor David Martin, who was one of six guests entertained by the Queen and Prince Philip at Buckingham Palace—"She looked tired and the corgis were jumping up and down."

The number of books written or edited by David Martin—on pacifism, religion, education—has mounted steadily during the years from 1965 onwards.

1968 Switzerland

1969 Switzerland

1971 Dordogne, France

The fruits of success

David Martin's distinguished professional career has been accompanied by a happy and rewarding family life. He met and married his wife Bernice—also a sociologist, and from a working class background—in 1962, when he was a lecturer at the London School of Economics. The financial rewards of his continuing hard work have enabled him to give his wife and children a privileged life that includes such pleasures as the foreign holidays recorded above—which his own hardworking parents would have considered unthinkably extravagant. In 1974, David Martin moved his family to a 16th-century half-timbered house at Woking in Surrey —the epitome of peaceful, middle-class comfort.

Professor David Martin gathers his wife Bernice and his children—Jonathan, Jessica, Izaak and Magnus—for a family photograph at their Surrey home.

1972 Ireland

1973 French Pyrenees

1974 Spain

The Martins' home is a rambling Elizabethan mansion of great charm—and value—within commuting distance of central London.

The Rule Breakers

4

"If a man does not keep pace with his companions, perhaps it is because he hears a different drummer", wrote Henry David Thoreau in 1854 in *Walden*. Educated at Harvard, Thoreau spent several years teaching in Concord, Massachusetts, and then decided to go off and live by himself in a cabin on the banks of near-by Walden Pond—to fish, hoe beans, watch the flight of hawks, and write books and essays in praise of nonconformity. "The greater part of what my neighbours call good I believe in my soul to be bad," said Thoreau, "and if I repent of anything, it is very likely to be my good behaviour."

Thoreau's kind of nonconformity is referred to by social scientists as deviance, the tendency to break the rules of society and go a separate way. In varying degrees, this tendency is present in all men. It becomes evident when people cross the street against the light, park over time, litter the roadside with cigarette wrappers and soft-drink cans, leave hotels with "souvenir" towels tucked into their luggage. This deviant behaviour takes a more serious form when people refuse to pay their taxes or object to serving in their country's armed forces.

For society is built upon the premise that people will conform. To achieve its objectives, it sets definite goals and values for its members, things that it regards as worth striving for. It also defines the means by which these goals are to be achieved. "Every social group invariably couples its cultural objectives with regulations, rooted in the mores or institutions, of allowable procedures for moving towards these objectives," explained sociologist Robert Merton of Columbia University. These regulations and procedures must be adhered to if the social structure and the status system are to remain intact.

Society spells out its regulations and procedures by what Edwin Lemert of the University of California called positive and negative norms. Positive norms say what an individual must do; they define the kinds of behaviour society esteems and honours. Negative norms tell him what he may not do; they warn him of activities that are forbidden.

Although all societies set up a mixture of the norms, one or the other generally dominates. The feudal societies of the Middle Ages were largely organized around positive norms, stipulating in explicit detail how people worked, played and worshipped. Most modern Western societies are based upon negative norms that prohibit certain actions but leave the rest up to personal choice.

In a stable society, most people conform to the positive or negative norms; some even obey so compulsively that they exceed the normal range of behaviour and by their exaggerated conformity become non-conformists. Thus, anyone so concerned with meeting standards for neatness that he constantly brushes his clothes and rearranges his hair is, to most people, at least a little odd; minor deviations from the norm are considered normal, and their lack becomes abnormal. But beyond such unconscious nonconformity is a more deliberate violation of the norms. Almost invariably there are those who refuse to go along. They may do so because they do not fully understand or accept the goals. Or they may accept the goals, but insist on their own means of attaining them. Or they may reject the whole status system, and drop out of society or try to alter it radically.

The ranks of nonconformists include rebels, renegades, criminals, alcoholics, hippies, hermits, creative artists, scientific geniuses, intellectuals and individualists—everybody who at one time or another goes against the grain of those around them.

Society's reaction to these violations of its norms ranges from tolerant amusement to outright alarm. When Albert Einstein chose to go sockless because "socks, you know, get holes in them—my wife does nothing but mend them", he was accepted sockless in the highest levels of society. Similarly, Britons admired philosopher Herbert Spencer despite his daily habit of stopping his carriage, even in the busy traffic of Piccadilly Circus, to check the state of his pulse.

Einstein and Spencer both benefited from what social psychologists call an idiosyncrasy credit. The achievements of the two men had built up a reservoir of good will towards them. "Idiosyncrasy credit," wrote psychologists Edward Jones and Harold Gerard, "is made up of the sum of the positive dispositions of the others toward the person. These credits are bestowed on him as rewards for meeting the expectations of the other group members or taken away if he fails to meet their expectations. The greater his accumulation of credit the higher the person's status is and the more he is accepted by others."

On the other hand, Oscar Wilde, who was esteemed as one of the finest playwrights of the 19th century, found himself in serious trouble for overstepping society's tolerance for sexual deviance—even though as a literary artist he had acquired a considerable sum of idiosyncrasy credit, and society allowed him broad behavioural latitude in other respects. Homosexuality at that time was considered to be such a threat to the values of society that his credit became overdrawn, so to speak, and as a result he was sent to jail.

When sociologists talk of nonconformity, they are concerned mainly with threats to society's accepted norms. They speak of "deviant behaviour", and have in mind criminals, drug addicts, revolutionaries, alcoholics and dropouts—people who behave negatively from society's point of view. Yet nonconformity should not be thought of simply as a pejorative term. In its fullest sense, the concept includes those who want to improve or remake society and its values as well as those who tend to tear it down—the innovators and the geniuses as well as those who are usually included under the heading of deviant.

Nonconformity may stem either from an inability or an unwillingness to conform to society's demands. As defined by the sociologists, it has two major sources. The first is strain, resulting from the intellectual or emotional burden of conforming. The second is "faulty socialization" —a failure to learn or abide by the norms expected by the society in which a person finds himself. This failure may stem from inadequate socialization: for example, a child misbehaves at a party for the simple reason that he has not yet been taught the behaviour expected of him.

The socialization may be inappropriate: the norms that the individual has learned may not apply in the situation in which he finds himself. This often occurs when conflicting cultures come together, as happens more and more frequently in a world in which Pakistanis staff London hotels, Turks work in German factories and Spaniards make up whole villages in France.

Such a clash between cultures having different values led to the famous Case of the Turbans. In Britain in 1959 an Indian Sikh, Gyani Sundar Singh Sagar, got a job as a bus conductor and insisted on wearing his turban instead of the grey cap prescribed by his employer, Manchester City Transport. Although he explained that the turban was worn for religious resons, and had been for 500 years, the Transport committee would not hear of such nonconformity. "If turbans are permitted, there is nothing to prevent other conductors and drivers with a whole string of religious beliefs turning up to work with all sorts of badges or devices", one committee member said.

It took an editorial in the Manchester *Guardian*, a thousand-word document from the local Sikh temple, pointing to the war record of turban-clad Sikh regiments in Britain's many wars, and a sharp letter from a *Guardian* reader to make Manchester City Transport change its mind. "Is it not a queer commentary on our social system," inquired the reader, "that we spend good money chasing around the world looking at local costumes, many of which are no longer worn under normal conditions but are merely displayed for the benefit of tourists —and yet, when a genuine variation from our habitual dress appears, bureaucracy has to raise its ugly head to stamp it out?"

But the question of whether or not a Sikh's turban was acceptable headgear did not end there. In 1969, still another Sikh, Sohan Singh Jolly went to work for the Wolverhampton Transport Committee; it was no more willing than Manchester City Transport to let him wear his turban and beard to work, and gave in only after he threatened to burn himself to death. And in 1975, Baldev Singh Chahal was sentenced to prison for a month for riding his motorbike wearing his turban instead

of the crash helmet that is required by British law. Chahal had been booked more than 37 times since the law went into effect, and had been fined innumerable times but had refused to pay. "I am quite prepared to go to prison," he said. "Just tell me the time and place to turn up." The British courts complied, and Chahal spent 30 days in prison. But the case for nonconformity was not lost. The possibility that wearing a turban might become acceptable later emerged when a bill was introduced in Parliament that would allow the exemption of turban-wearing Sikhs from the crash-helmet law.

The Case of the Turbans became a cause célèbre despite the fact that the British have a reputation for being a tolerant people in most matters, including peculiarities of dress. The Sikhs could wear their turbans on the streets of Manchester or Wolverhampton, and even to work in most jobs, and no one cared. It was only when the turban-wearing of Sikh culture came into conflict with goals important in British culture —highway safety, uniform requirements for transport workers—that trouble occurred.

Nonconformity that arises from cultural diversity is given wide latitude in most modern societies—but only up to the point at which it threatens the deeply held values of the majority. This capacity to let people deviate freely until they pose a threat to society has enabled one "inappropriately socialized" group in America, the Amish, to live in peace for many years.

The Amish are a religious sect that originated in central Europe in the 17th century and fled to America to escape persecution for their heretical views. They believe that God wants man to live as simply as possible, to keep himself "unspotted from the world". In their pursuit of unworldliness the Amish refuse to wear bright colours, they fasten their clothing with press-studs—because buttons are considered ornaments —and they have standardized their dress to a uniform. Men wear black suits with uncreased trousers; sweaters are forbidden because they are too form-fitting. The hem of a woman's dress must be no higher than 20 centimetres from the floor and the dress itself must always be covered by an apron. Except when she goes to bed at night, a woman's hair is covered by a bonnet-like cap. The Amish home is equally devoid of fripperies; it contains no decorations whatsoever—no mirrors, no pictures, no upholstered furniture. Linoleum and oilcloth are permitted but may not be patterned; and windows may be shaded only with dark-green blinds. There is, naturally, no telephone, no electricity, no radio, no TV. In fact, there is no music, except for singing—and even then, the Amish avoid the insidious pleasure of singing in harmony.

Outside the home, the Amish determination not to be lured into the

Wheeling across Piccadilly Circus wearing the crew-cut hair that is their badge of nonconformity, four British working-class "skinheads" eye their opposition, a group of typically long-haired young people. Ironically, not many years before, long hair, rather than short, was considered unconventional.

"Satanic Kingdom" results in behaviour equally austere. While almost everyone else in 20th-century industrial society has converted to the automobile, the Amish continue to ride in horse-drawn carriages. And though an occasional Amish farmer will own a tractor or rent a mechanized cutter-loader to prepare silage for his cows, in the main the sect frowns on "the drift into modern things" on the land as well as in the home. Indeed, the *ordnung*, or rules, of one Amish community specifically state that tractors are permissible only for tasks that cannot be done with horses—and that tractors, even when used, must be fitted with steel treads. No air-filled rubber tyres are allowed.

Hard-working, sober ("We don't read in the Bible of Christ laughing"), disdaining most of the social graces that smooth ordinary human encounters (please and thank you are words seldom heard in everyday Amish conversation), the Amish are nevertheless tolerated and even admired by most of their neighbours. "They're wonderful people to live among", says one non-Amish neighbour. Yet when the Amish have challenged a basic American value, tolerance for them has eroded. Until 1972, when a U.S. Supreme Court decision ruled in their favour on the grounds of religious freedom, the Amish were frequently harassed by authorities for refusing, in line with their commitment to the simple life, to send their children to school beyond the eighth grade—the age of 13.

The other broad source of nonconformity—after faulty socialization—is strain. For some people, the burden of understanding society's conflicting norms or its values and objectives is too great. They may find that compliance is beyond their capacity. They may subscribe to society's goals but find themselves unable to follow the prescribed routes for attaining them, or they may reject the entire social system—both its goals and its prescribed forms of behaviour. Robert Merton divided strain-induced nonconformity into four distinct categories: innovation, ritualism, retreatism and rebellion.

The innovator accepts his culture's goals, but decides that he can reach the goals only by an unconventional route. The bank embezzler, for example, fervently subscribes to the socially approved goal of financial success, but he chooses a nonconformist route to achieve it. On a more elevated level, the great astronomer Copernicus was an innovator. He pursued a culturally approved goal in his efforts towards understanding the cosmos, but then deviated by looking to the skies rather than to the Scriptures for guidance.

The ritualist takes the opposite tack. He conforms to the means of achieving the goal with such obsessive care that he never gets where he wants to go. The officious bureaucrat is a classic example. In his

continued on page 122

In the portal of a Greek temple, a toga-draped Isadora Duncan adopts a worshipful stance. Her tempestuous life and disregard for classic techniques in her dancing shocked her contemporaries.

Art and the bohemian life

"Be orderly and regular in your life, like a bourgeois," French novelist Flaubert cautioned, "so that you may be wild and original in your work." Flaubert's advice—which he himself heeded—contradicts the general notion of the innovator in the arts as a nonconformist in personal behaviour.

Many avant-garde artists have indeed been bohemians. Isadora Duncan (*right*) had a succession of lovers; Picasso had two wives and five mistresses, who bore him four legitimate and illegitimate children; George Sand, a French baroness, took a man's name in 1832 to pursue what was then a man's career as an author. But many others, like Flaubert, lived lives as pedestrian as their work was avant-garde. And the furore aroused by unconventional art or life style has been short-lived. When Igor Stravinsky's *The Rite of Spring* was first presented in 1913, the composer was hissed and booed for his "radical" ballet. Today the work is a classic.

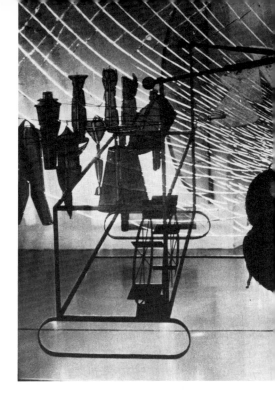

Marcel Duchamp ponders his controversial glass-and-metal creation enigmatically titled The Bride Stripped Bare by Her Bachelors, Even. *A pioneer of modern art—his painting* Nude Descending a Staircase *shocked American audiences in 1913—he was an all-around iconoclast; in 1923 he abruptly abandoned art and spent most of his remaining 45 years quietly playing chess.*

In her Paris studio, Gertrude Stein looks up as her friend Alice B. Toklas enters the room. Stein's abandonment of such conventions as punctuation and plot influenced modern literature; at home, her lifelong relationship with Toklas was equally nonconformist.

The flamboyant Oscar Wilde strikes an effete pose in the
velvet jacket and knee breeches he insisted on wearing.
His nonconformist behaviour was not reflected in his work
—conventional 19th-century society comedies—
but it resulted in his trial and subsequent imprisonment
for sodomy, and it scandalized Victorian England.

Buckminster Fuller, who ranks among the century's most
radical architects and inventors, stands in front of
one of his famous geodesic domes. He was kicked out of
Harvard for "general irresponsibility", but he settled down
to a prolific career and a long, happy marriage.

preoccupation with details of procedures and regulations, he may prevent the achievement that the rules are intended to facilitate.

The retreatist simply opts out. He is, in Merton's words, "*In* the society, but not *of* it". He may be a drug addict, or an alcoholic or even a hermit who has withdrawn from society for philosophic reasons, like Henry Thoreau.

The rebel not only rejects the social structure and all its values, like the retreatist, but sets out to alter it to suit his own ideas. He may be a political radical, bent on changing the system, or an avant-garde artist, determined to change the canons of his art. He poses the most serious threat to the status system or group, because he wants to tear it down and build a completely different structure.

Individuals may find, in extreme cases of strain, that a society has failed to set up norms they can follow without severe internal conflicts. Instead of telling the individual how to behave, society sometimes presents him with a multiplicity of choices, no two in agreement. Torn between contradictory signals, damned if he does and damned if he does not, he fails to conform because he has no standard to measure his conduct against. The norms have in effect cancelled one another. This condition, which social scientists call anomie, or normlessness, is a particular problem for large, complex urban societies where the composition of the population changes rapidly and many sorts of people and cultural influences are constantly coming together.

While it is blamed for the deviant behaviour of many big-city juvenile delinquents, anomie also has other less noticeable victims. Among them are those people who go through all of the motions of conformity, who appear to have confidence in the system, but actually live without values. There is nothing in the system that commands their respect or allegiance. They live by rote, and many of them lead lives of desperation, drowning their lack of commitment at the end of the day in too many beers or martinis. However, the confusion may not originate with the individual. One sociologist has even suggested that the multiple norms of modern society make the very idea of deviance meaningless: if society cannot offer its members a way to distinguish between good and evil, right and wrong, proper and improper behaviour, how can there be such a thing as nonconformity?

All of these types of nonconformists have been irritants to their less adventurous fellow men throughout history. But in recent decades the strongest challenge to established status systems has come from the retreatists and rebels. Both of these groups have been dissatisfied with the goals and the prescribed behaviour of their cultures. The student radicals of the 1960s wanted to tear down the whole structure of society. Many of them were not sure about what they wanted to put up in its place, but they were rebelling en masse against the goals and values of the society around them.

The other large nonconformist group was the hippies, who in Merton's lexicon were retreatists. Like the rebels they rejected everything that society stood for. But their solution was to withdraw. And in the process—like many nonconformist groups—they became little islands of conformity within the culture they were rejecting.

The hippies proclaimed their antipathy to the social values of their parents by adopting startlingly different life styles. In Germany, where cleanliness is a particular virtue, the hippie, or *Gammler*, went unwashed and dishevelled. In America, despite especially severe sanctions against the use of drugs, hippies "freaked out" on pot, hashish, LSD and amphetamines—or worse. Systematically opposing the standards of their middle-class upbringing, hippies wore their hair long; dressed like the poor in drab, patched clothes; spoke in the language of the ghetto; repudiated the idea of routine jobs and productive work; and forswore personal privacy to live in the casual extended family of the commune or the crash pad. But despite their refusal to follow the norms of the society at large, the hippies set up norms of their own. In the places where hippies congregated, such as the *provo* section of Amsterdam or the Haight-Ashbury section of San Francisco, a curious sort of uniformity was visible—everyone seemed to be dressed the same, to be high on drugs and to be living on hand-outs.

Some communes were authoritarian, taking their direction from a spiritual guru. Other communes were leaderless; they regulated their affairs by consensus, either spontaneously or in long-drawn-out "rap sessions". Some communes had work schedules, committees, treasurers and weekly allowances; others prided themselves on functioning amateurishly—their members worked when the spirit moved them and did not even share common meal times. Diet was usually an important element of the commune's philosophy, but the diet also varied from one commune to another. Some farming communes kept cows, chickens and goats, while others would have nothing to do with animal products. The Shrubb family in Norfolk, and the Towey community in Wales practised vegetarianism; the New Buffalo pueblo commune in the American Southwest existed on an Indian diet of sweet corn, beans and an occasional poached deer.

But while communes varied greatly from one to another, most of them had one thing in common besides their rejection of the outer world. They were rigidly conformist within their own confines, and

Heads newly shaved and their customary Western garb abandoned for saffron robes, German initiates into the Hare Krishna sect dance on the lawn of Rettershof Castle to celebrate their adoption of a life style at odds with the one followed by most of their compatriots.

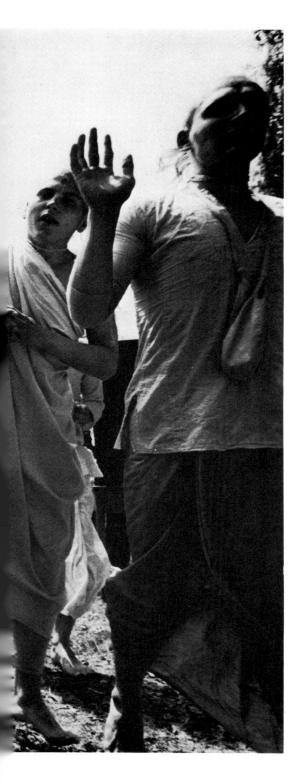

their tolerance for nonconformity was limited.

Somewhat akin to the hippie communards in their rejection of conventional values is another group of retreatists: disaffected individuals who backed down the status ladder, but did not withdraw from society completely. In the affluent society of upper-middle-class America in the 1970s, were a surprising number of young people who left the professions for which they were educated in order to work at manual jobs. Expressing their discontent with the desk-bound life of their fathers, they embarked on a path of what sociologists would call "downward mobility", to work as piano movers, fork-lift operators, plumbers, carpenters and builders. Michael Krich, brought up in the fashionable suburb of Short Hills, New Jersey, bought himself an 18-wheel tractor-trailer and became a truck driver. Jerry Kier, with a masters degree in geology from Duke University, left a teaching job at the University of Texas to become a house painter. Judy Rolle, who described herself as a former "prissy schoolteacher", oiled heavy machinery standing up to her knees in muck on the Alaska pipeline. Though their manual labour lowered the status of these young people, most seemed to take a kind of pride in this movement down the ladder.

Often, the motives of nonconformists are mixed. They do not fit neatly into the categories set up by Merton. Almost everyone except a member of a nudist colony would agree that nudists are nonconformists. Yet they do not all take off their clothes for the same reasons. Some might be considered innovators, pursuing the goal of good health —by a deviant means—while others are rebels, challenging the values of the rest of the world.

Like many other nonconformists, nudists are remarkably conformist when they are among themselves. In a study of social nudism in 1971, sociologist William Hartman of California State University discovered that the maintenance of a nudist colony's way of life apparently depended on rules, strict but unwritten, that were observed by almost everyone. No alcohol was allowed, and there was no body contact. Not even husbands and wives were permitted to walk hand in hand or drape their arms over each other's shoulders. Prolonged staring was also considered very bad form unless the stare was eye-to-eye, and the nudists prided themselves on their ability to maintain eye contact.

This insistence on specified norms of behaviour may have helped change the popular view of social nudism; once judged as both daring and lewd, it came to be considered acceptable. By the mid-1970s social nudism was spreading and steadily becoming less controversial, and its practitioners were seen as avant-garde, the nonconformists who lead society towards new forms of behaviour. At the "Celebration of Life" rock concert in McCrea, Louisiana, in 1971, thousands of young people removed their clothes in a display so massive that local police were powerless to deal with it. In West Germany there were approximately one million practitioners of *Freikörperkultur* (literally, free body culture). Regularly every summer the FKKs descended in swarms on the German island of Sylt, on the Ile du Levant off the French Riviera, on Corsica and the Spanish island of Ibiza, and most especially on the Adriatic coast of Yugoslavia. There the favourite resort was Valalta, a 60-hectare compound with three guarded "sunning meadows", a beautician and a supermarket. "One of the greatest thrills in the world," observed an American actress who spent two weeks in a European nudist resort, "is pushing a grocery cart naked in the supermarket". Nudism, which once had been a shocking form of nonconformity, was on the way towards gaining broad acceptance.

Acceptance is one way that society reacts to nonconformity. But deviance is difficult for any culture to take to its bosom. Because there are always some standards of behaviour that people are expected to conform to, there are always certain kinds of conduct that are taboo. Violence may be condoned in some cultures, but the murder of a neighbour is condemned everywhere. And although sexual practices vary exotically, some form of incest—intercourse of a son with his mother, a daughter with her father or between other close kin—is taboo in every culture that is known to social scientists. Except for these two universal taboos, different times and different places have seen an extraordinary range of human behaviour countenanced or forbidden, and an extraordinary number of ways have been devised for dealing with the individuals who practised the deviant behaviour.

Witches and heretics have been burned at the stake, drowned and buried alive. Unfaithful wives have been stoned to death. Galileo was forced by the Inquisition to recant for contending that the earth revolved around the sun. And Socrates was compelled to commit suicide for corrupting the minds of Athenian youths with questions about the values of Athenian society.

Sometimes the punishment meted out by a hostile society to its nonconforming members is difficult to fathom. In the Soviet Union many people who have expressed opinions that are contrary to those approved by society have been committed to mental institutions. In one sense the confinement is probably intended purely as punishment. Like prison, the detention removes the offending individual from the social scene and prevents him from contaminating the rest of society—in this case, with his ideas. But in the Soviet Union the very act of questioning the moral code or of insisting on freedom of speech is regarded quite literally as demented behaviour. The nuclear physicist Andrei Sakharov, whose courage in championing human rights in the Soviet Union won him the Nobel Prize for Peace in 1975, on occasion referred to himself ironically as Andrei Blazhenny—*blazhenny* being the Russian word for crazy mixed-up saint.

Though punishment is the most obvious way society handles its deviant individuals, it is not the only way. Far more pervasive—and probably more effective, too—are the mechanisms society uses to absorb the nonconforming individual into the system and make him a part of the mainstream of society. Sometimes these mechanisms operate unconsciously; society is not aware of the social conditioning it imposes and neither is the individual who participates in it. Thus, the settlement houses set up in New York and Chicago in the early days of the 20th century, ostensibly to smooth the transition of European immigrants into American society, actually served another purpose as well. By teaching the ambitious immigrant to read and write English, giving him a trade and indoctrinating him in the norms of American life, such pioneer social workers as Jane Addams and her Hull House colleagues were in effect de-fusing a potentially explosive minority that could have upset the American status quo.

In all societies, altruistic scholarships and training programmes aiming to improve the lot of the lower classes have the same effect. By taking bright people out of depressed levels and enabling them to find a way up the status ladder, these philanthropic efforts pre-empt the lower levels' natural leaders, who might become activist nonconformists opposed to the goals and values of the establishment. Once these people have climbed into the establishment levels, they frequently have become ardent conformists themselves.

Even when total absorption is impossible, society has ingenious ways of coming to terms with nonconformity. Anthropologists who were studying American Indian societies discovered that among the Cheyenne, homosexuals were permitted to remain homosexuals, and their deviant behaviour was neatly dovetailed into the structure of tribal life. The *berdache*, or man-woman, dressed in women's clothes and performed routine tasks similar to those of the women of the tribe. In addition, he was often the medicine man of the tribe, revered and respected for his knowledge of cures and spells. Indeed, the Cheyenne believed that no girl could resist the special power of the love potions made up by a *berdache*. This same curative and magical skill made the *berdache* a valued member of war parties. But warriors also appreciated his presence because his unused maleness was thought to increase

127

the warriors' virility—functioning rather like money in the bank.

Less exotic than the Cheyenne treatment of tribal nonconformists, but stemming from the same kind of concern, were the flexible hours introduced by some corporations in Western Europe and the United States to accommodate the varying life styles of their employees. An insurance company in New York, for example, allowed its employees in some divisions to work a three-day week of two 12-hour days and one 11-hour day and then have the rest of the week off. Other divisions, whose employees were needed on the premises during the standard working week, worked a five-day week, but the employees were permitted to set the starting and finishing hours.

Some nonconformism is accepted as normal in society because it is expected, as if more conventional people required it in order to exist. The painters, writers, musicians and poets who form bohemian sub-cultures traditionally have been more or less permanently at variance with the remainder of society.

Jazz musicians in the early 1950s, as sociologist Howard Becker pointed out in an article, lived lives sufficiently unconventional and bizarre for them to be labelled outsiders. They felt themselves mysteriously gifted. No one, as one trombone player put it, could "teach a guy to have a beat; either he's got one or he hasn't". From this it followed that no one could tell a musician how to do anything else, either, and therefore he did not feel bound to abide by society's conventions. In fact, he delighted in flouting them, in doing whatever came into his head, the madder and more devil-may-care the better—and society seemed to respect him for this attitude. "You know," said one jazz musician, "the biggest heroes in the music business are the biggest characters. The crazier a guy acts, the greater he is, the more everyone likes him." Some of this nonconformity was probably an attempt to ritualize what the musician felt to be his isolation from the world. Constantly on the move, working late into the night, he had little opportunity to make contact with people outside his profession. According to one young musician, in fact, musicians "talk a special language, dress different, and wear a different kind of glasses" simply to announce their differentness.

No matter how strange or difficult nonconformists may seem, they can be ignored or discounted only at society's peril. For creativity and human progress are largely the work of people who refuse to be bound by custom or tradition. Moreover, nonconformists who are reviled today may be revered tomorrow. "In the history of every society," says Robert Merton, "some of its culture heroes have been regarded as heroic precisely because they have had the courage and the vision to depart from norms then obtaining in the group. . . . The rebel,

A hippie stretches out in his sleeping bag, rucksack at his side, in the rotunda of Munich's English Garden, a favourite hangout. A few metres away, but immeasurably removed from his spirit of social defiance, two neatly dressed women admire the view, framed by graffiti-inscribed pillars.

129

revolutionary, nonconformist, individualist, heretic or renegade of an earlier time is often the culture hero of today."

One heretic who became a culture hero was the naturalist Charles Darwin, who was reviled and ridiculed in his own day for suggesting that all forms of life upon earth were descended from a single common source and were the product of an endless process of mutation. When Darwin first presented his publisher with the manuscript for *On the Origin of Species*, he was gently advised to abandon the project and write instead a book on his "observations on pigeons", which would be "curious, ingenious and valuable to the highest degree. Everybody is interested in pigeons".

When Darwin's book eventually was published, he faced a barrage of criticism from the press, the public, the pulpit—even from his own fellow scientists. "I did not feel that the slightest light could be thrown on my practical life for me, by having it ever so logically made out that my first ancestor, millions of ages back, had been, or even had not been, an oyster", wrote Mrs. Thomas Carlyle. Anti-Darwin scientists, clerics and laymen, mixing their disbelief with moral outrage, labelled his theory "utterly false and grievously mischievous", "a dreary discourse . . . full of morbid views of creation", and "absolutely incompatible with the revealed word of God". One geologist later recalled that when he was a student he had been forced to debate Darwin's theory with a friend in secret, "for to be caught at it," he said, "was to be detected in a careful study of a heresy".

Darwin was essentially a modest man with no taste for controversy. Bewildered by the virulence of the attacks, and at one point unable to face a particularly antagonistic gathering (he begged off by departing for a water cure, saying his stomach had "utterly broken down"), he nevertheless steadfastly defended the validity of his theory, and tried to be philosophical. "I have made up my mind to be well abused," he wrote in a letter to a friend, "but I think it of importance that my notions should be read by intelligent men, accustomed to scientific argument, though *not* naturalists. It may seem absurd, but I think such men will drag after them those naturalists who have too firmly fixed in their heads that a species is an entity." Ultimately, of course, he was proven right. By the time he died in 1882, Darwinian theory was on its way to becoming the new scientific orthodoxy, and Darwin himself—with Parliament's approval—was buried beside Sir Isaac Newton in Westminster Abbey. He was welcomed, in the words of one eulogy, into England's "band of gentle heroes".

A similar hero's end came to another renegade who lived through years of ostracism and abuse only to have his ideas accepted and finally become the cornerstone of a new conformity. When the French painter Edouard Manet had a first showing of his famous *Déjeuner sur l'herbe* at the Salon des Refusés in 1863, it was greeted with howls of derision. Paintings, according to French academic tradition, were supposed to be idealized renderings of scenes from antiquity or the Bible, or classical studies of the nude. It was perfectly all right, as one dissident Frenchman put it, to paint the sands of ancient Egypt but certainly not a cow pasture in Normandy. Manet upset this tradition by choosing as his subject a group of picnickers, the men wearing ordinary street clothes, the women naked—but not classically so. In short, they were real people. Worse yet, they were painted in brilliant colours that were laid on the canvas side by side, without any attempt to shade them into one another in conventional tones.

Déjeuner sur l'herbe and its successors made Manet famous, but famous in a way he never meant to be. He was branded as an unbalanced, uncultured rebel, as a "young man who paints with ink and constantly drops the inkwell", as "the apostle of the ugly and repulsive". One critic accused him of being "unable to draw carefully" and of

painting "dislocated figures awkwardly and painfully". "An epidemic of crazy laughter", noted another commentator, prevails "in front of the canvases by Manet." Indeed, the jeering mob at one exhibition became so hostile that the management had to assign special guards to protect Manet's paintings from damage.

Even his person was reviled. People stared at him on the street and in public places as though, wrote his friend Theodore Duret, he was some sort of "curious beast", an attention that was due solely, Duret said, to his reputation "as a madman, a barbarian who committed outrages in the domain of art and trampled under foot the traditions that were the glorious heritage of the nation".

Manet was totally unprepared for any of this. In fact, apart from his revolutionary art, he was not a rebel at all, but a very proper bourgeois gentleman. Sober in his habits, correct in his dress and bearing, known and appreciated among his circle of friends for his refinement, his polished manners and his lively wit, Manet wanted nothing more than

In flagrant nonconformity with Army regulations, two black American soldiers greet a passing officer with the upraised fist of the black power salute. This deviation, which occurred in Germany in 1970 at the height of the black power movement, was not tolerated by the Army; the two men were reprimanded.

to be accepted by society for the good painter he knew himself to be. "M. Manet has never wished to protest", he once said of himself.

In time the recognition came. His work was seen and admired by a group of younger artists—Cézanne, Berthe Morisot, Renoir, Monet, Sisley. Adopting him as their leader, they began to paint in his luminous colours and to follow his practice of painting directly from nature, in the open air. By 1874, they had coalesced into the group that came to be known as Impressionists, and a new art style had replaced the old. "In twenty years the methods, subjects, the whole system of aesthetics had been revolutionised," Theodore Duret wrote, "and Manet was its initiator." No longer excluded from the Salon of the French Académie Royale, which had for so long refused to hang his work, Manet was awarded the Salon medal in 1881. A year later the French government awarded him the Legion of Honour.

As well as providing society with its heroes, however, the nonconforming members of a group are, in the opinion of many social scientists, essential to the health of any society. Sociologist Robert Park spoke of the nonconformist as "the individual with the wider horizon, the keener intelligence, the more detached and rational viewpoint . . . the relatively more civilized human being". And Robert Merton noted that the nonconforming minority in a society frequently "represents the interest and ultimate values of the group more effectively than the conforming majority". Because he is a marginal person, living outside the mainstream of his society, the nonconformist is often able to transcend the group and see patterns and possibilities for making it better. This transcendence, in the opinion of Charles Willie of Harvard's Graduate School of Education, is as valuable to society as conformity. "We must consider the urge for freedom and change in people as well as the need for control and stability; the desire to try new things as well as to conform to the old." Willie concluded: "We must be on the look-out for the strain toward transcendence in human nature".

Gypsies: outsiders everywhere

Travelling much as their forefathers did centuries ago, a small band of Gypsies rides through the Greek countryside. Though some Gypsies have become sedentary, most of them remain nomads.

PHOTOGRAPHED BY HANS SILVESTER

Probably the most persistent nonconformists in history are the Gypsies. Ever since the 14th century, when in a mysterious migration these nomadic people from India began entering Europe, they have generally withstood pressure to become assimilated into other societies. Today, eight million strong, they remain resolutely apart from established social structures. They are scattered over every continent but live mainly in Europe, linked to one another by their own customs and language, Romany.

According to anthropologist Anne Sutherland, the key to the Gypsies' ability to hold on to their separateness lies in the sharp boundary they maintain between themselves and non-Gypsies. To keep it, the Gypsy deliberately limits relations with *gaje*—outsiders. He earns his living from the *gaje*, working as an itinerant coppersmith, mechanic, farm labourer—or confidence man. But he avoids social contacts or genuine friendships, hiding behind his ethnic stereotype to discourage any *gaje* from getting too close (*pages 142-143*).

Equally important in the preservation of this boundary, according to expert Jan Yoors, is a Gypsy paradox: to outsiders Gypsies are the world's foremost nonconformists, but within their own group they are strict conformists. Their behaviour, from relations between the sexes to washing and eating habits, is rigidly determined by an elaborate social code called the *romania*. Anyone who breaks the code may be banished, forced to live among the *gaje*. Since the code also stigmatizes the *gaje* as morally and even physically corrupt, every Gypsy carefully honours the rules of the *romania* in order to avoid the exile from his own people that, to him, is a punishment equal to death.

Puffing expertly, a Gypsy youngster in Canada narrows his eyes against tobacco smoke. From infancy on, the children of the Gypsies are given cigarettes the way other children are given sweets.

A blanket, which is slung over two ropes attached to caravans, forms a cradle for a sleeping baby whose care has been delegated to a young Gypsy girl.

Following the nomadic way of life

Nomadism has led Gypsies into a casually improvised life style—"They at all times give the impression of camping temporarily," noted Jean-Paul Clébert, the French writer on Gypsy life. This style handily survives efforts to force conformity to *gaje* ideas; when Czechoslovak officials settled Gypsies into brand-new flats, the Gypsies took the stoves outside, used doors for firewood, and cooked and dined alfresco. But nomadic improvisation imposes adult responsibilities—and habits—on the young as much as it nurtures a free and easy independence of spirit.

A simple tent is home to a family on the
road in Greece. Gypsies are extremely
adept at erecting tents with whatever
material the locale provides: tree
branches and bark, rushes and reeds. But
the fact that their structures are
often flimsy has given rise to a Gypsy
name for the wind: the devil's sneeze.

A family gathers around a simmering pot
—one of two daily meals eaten when
on the move. Typically, the food consists
of vegetables, from the countryside,
and fowl from nearby farms, all washed
down with water from a stream.

Carrying out his duties as leader, a Gypsy chief orders a clan member to prepare for an annual prilgrimage to the South of France (pages 144-145), a centuries-old Roman Catholic tradition adopted by the Gypsies only in recent decades.

Gypsy women leave their hair uncombed and sustain themselves with coffee while lamenting a dead matriarch. During this first phase of the mourning ritual, which lasts for several days, the men go unwashed and unshaven, and drink beer or wine—only the children eat.

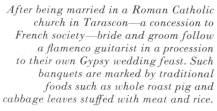

After being married in a Roman Catholic church in Tarascon—a concession to French society—bride and groom follow a flamenco guitarist in a procession to their own Gypsy wedding feast. Such banquets are marked by traditional foods such as whole roast pig and cabbage leaves stuffed with meat and rice.

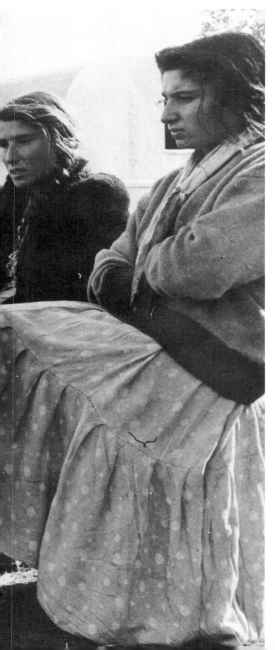

Customs to preserve a culture

Through the centuries, the distinctive customs of the Gypsies have helped them maintain their identity as a special group. Many of these traditions regulate experiences basic to all human life: marriage is always arranged by the fathers, and ideally is celebrated by a three-day banquet. Death must take place in the open—necessitating the removal outdoors of dying Gypsies—and is followed by a full year of commemorative feasts.

Enforcement of these customs is entrusted to one man who emerges as a leader. Behind his authority lies the *kris*, a body of unwritten law administered by a council of elders who can punish violators of tradition.

An omen that greets Gypsies all across France is signs like this one reading "Nomads Forbidden". It was erected by the police, who have the power to decide where Gypsies may or may not rest. However, the woman's slip hung over a wire near the sign suggests that a caravan has decided to ignore the warning.

Paying the price of being different

In all societies nonconformists tend to be scapegoats, and Gypsies have suffered cruel persecution, including periodic attempts at genocide. In 1561, a French parliament ordered them exterminated "by steel and by fire", and in 1725, Frederick William I of Prussia decreed the hanging of all adult Gypsies. In the 20th century, the Nazis executed over 400,000 Gypsies.

Even when they are not threatened by atrocities, Gypsies face harassment, particularly restrictions on their freedom of movement. To fight such discrimination, the World Romany Congress, an international Gypsy group, has campaigned for the right to travel unimpeded throughout Europe.

Anxiously eyeing a gendarme, a Gypsy
family endures one of many identity
checks, submitting papers they are
required to carry while on the road in
France. Restrictions are tighter in Italy,
which has only seven camping sites,
and in Belgium, where the police try to
prevent any nomadic party from entering.

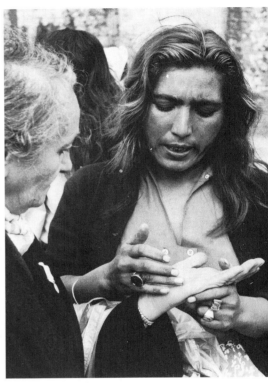

In their traditional role of mendicants, Gypsy women beg in the streets of a French town. Begging is unrelated to poverty; it is a common activity even among Gypsies who hoard gold coins—a favourite form of wealth—in a game to see who can collect the most money.

A Gypsy woman prophesies the future, practising an art intended exclusively for the gaje: Gypsies themselves do not believe in any type of fortune-telling.

Manipulating the gaje for fun and profit

Gypsies know perfectly well that the non-Gypsies they live among generally do not like them, but anthropologist Anne Sutherland found that this prejudice reinforces their traditional disdain for the gaje and their determination to get everything they can out of the outside world. They cynically adopt the stereotypes expected of them, acting as beggars, practitioners of the occult, street pedlars and confidence tricksters.

Sutherland pointed out that these roles enable Gypsies to turn a profit by exploiting the gullibility of the gaje, for Gypsies believe that it is immoral to earn money from one another. Such professions are also sufficiently unsavory to discourage most of the gaje from seeking out Gypsy companionship —and therefore assist in the creation of a screen behind which the entire Gypsy community can live.

*Offering—for a suitable contribution—to
break out of the chains that bind him,
a young Gypsy provides entertainment for
the* gaje *with an act that may be a hoax.*

Piously carrying a religious statue, massed Gypsies traipse through a field in the Camargue in France, on an annual pilgrimage they undertake more out of opportunism than spiritual zeal. Students of the culture believe the purpose of the pilgrimage is social. Since the police do not interfere with this ostensibly religious rite, it gives Gypsies from all over the world one chance a year to travel without harassment, meet with long-unseen friends and relatives, and conduct family business like finding brides for sons.

Overturning Old Ways

Plus ça change, plus c'est la même chose—the more things change, the more they remain the same—is a favourite cliché of English-speaking people who are putting on upper-class airs. Not many of them realize that the epigram originated as a comment on status itself. It was written by a now-almost-forgotten journalist of 19th-century France, Alphonse Karr, and was a perceptive analysis of one of the strangest facts about social stratification systems: they are always both constant and changing, creating, modifying, unmaking and re-creating positions within the social hierarchy.

Karr was a detached, often satirical observer of the in-again, out-again fortunes of ambitious status-seekers in the revolutionary turbulence that, at different times over two centuries, overturned old social systems in France, Russia (*left*) and China. Karr had a close-up view of the exciting aftermath of the French Revolution. It had destroyed one of the most rigid feudal hierarchies of Europe, a hierarchy that was composed by law of Three Estates. The mobs of Paris simply lopped off the First Estate and the heads of many of its members, the nobility, and forced the remnants to flee the country in disordered droves. The fervour for rationalism swept aside the Second Estate, the clergy, many of whom had to go into hiding. The situation left in power only the Third Estate —the people. But it was a muddled amalgam of a class, made up of shopkeepers, tradesmen, artisans, workers, peasants and street rabble. This unlikely mixture and the advent of the Reign of Terror produced chaos in the stratification system, but French society was soon galvanized under Napoleon. The conqueror of Europe replaced the republic with an empire, filling its highest positions with a newly created nobility who had rendered service to the state. But Napoleon, too, was to fall, along with his empire. The Allied victors restored the heirs of the decapitated Bourbon monarch Louis XVI.

The period of the Bourbon restoration brought back those nobles who had fled the Revolution, and they now competed with Napoleon's newly made aristocrats for wealth and honours. The clergy again rose to dominance. But the lower classes, who had tasted the rewards of an open society, also demanded that they be given increased privilege. The situation was explosive, culminating in the Paris Revolt of 1830 and the Second Republic. Power shifted towards the imperial nobility, away from the Church, and trickled slightly downwards to the people. Then Louis Napoleon swept aside the Republic and launched the Second Empire, which collapsed during the Franco-Prussian War. In the aftermath, it seemed to Karr that French society had simply gone full cycle back to 1789, and that the cycle seemed destined to go on interminably. In his later years, Karr stated that his simple epigram summed up his entire experience of politics and society; it was the culmination "of what I have read and what I have seen".

The accuracy of Karr's observation has been demonstrated repeatedly in the years since his day. Revolutions more violent than any he witnessed have toppled old regimes and instituted new systems in their place. In the industrialized nations economic and technological innovations have added innumerable rungs to the status ladder and have abruptly switched people up and down it. Political reforms such as death duties and progressive income taxes have helped redistribute wealth to enlarge the middle classes from the ranks of the very rich and the very poor. Mass education, which now extends to the university level, has eliminated many of the social distinctions that were formerly linked to schooling.

That such dramatic developments have altered status is obvious to almost anyone who compares his own life with that of his great-grandfather. And yet beneath many of these alterations can be discerned patterns that have remained remarkably stable over the ages. Revolutionaries who destroyed rigid systems of classifying people often substituted rigid systems of their own; the names of the players changed, but the game remained the same. Despite efforts to eliminate status entirely and create classless societies, new elites repeatedly rose to the surface, accompanied by all the perquisites of privilege and luxury— the Communist bureaucrat's shiny limousine, the African nationalist's Savile Row tailor, the newly created British peer's posh country manor in his Socialist-minded nation.

This paradox of constancy amid change has been explained in many ways. Some authorities traced social change to innate, poorly understood human instincts, such as a drive for power or aggression. Aristotle, more than 2,000 years ago, saw social struggle as a simple battle between the haves and have-nots, caused by "the desire of equality, when men think that they are equal to others who have more than themselves; or again the desire of inequality and superiority, when conceiving themselves to be superior they think that they have not more but the same or less than their inferiors". But modern scholars believe social change comes about as a result of the interplay of factors that are much more complex. They attribute the continual existence of efforts to restructure society to recurring conflicts between external circumstances and internal attitudes—between a society's struggle to survive (if possible, to prosper) and its concept of justice. Two quite different views were devised by the French evolutionist Emile Durkheim and the German revolutionary philosopher Karl Marx.

Durkheim believed that societies change in a way that parallels biological evolution. Just as natural organisms tend to become ever more differentiated and complex—beginning as single cells and moving upwards toward *Homo sapiens*—societies developed from simple bands of gatherers to the complex organization of modern industrial states. The key to the change in society, in Durkheim's view, was related to alterations in the division of human labour, which was continually expanding and becoming more elaborate.

In its most primitive form, this division of labour allocated tasks requiring physical strength, such as warfare and the hunt, to males, and the domestic chores of gathering food, child rearing and cooking to women. As societies became more advanced, the division of labour multiplied and branched into the immense number of specialized functions of a modern society. Ideally, the division of labour placed individuals in the social system according to their capacities to perform these functions. In practice, as Durkheim fully realized, societies behave "abnormally": factors such as caste and class often predetermine a person's position in the social scheme of things. Despite such inequalities, however, Durkheim postulated that increasing specialization arising from the division of labour makes individuals increasingly more dependent upon one another, and therefore helps to hold societies together.

The founding father of Marxism, on the other hand, believed in just the opposite. For Karl Marx, the tendency of societies is not towards solidarity, but towards continuous internal destruction. History in this interpretation is the story of societies being ripped asunder from within because of class strife, then rebuilding upon the resulting rubble a new order that contained the seeds of its own destruction. Like Durkheim, Marx believed that the most important single factor in this process is an individual's labour, which provides him the means through which to satisfy his needs and achieve self-realization. But Marx felt that work is dictated not by natural capacities but by competition for scarce resources and for control of the means of production. This competition divides mankind into two classes, consisting of the controllers and the controlled —the exploiters and the exploited, the haves and the have-nots. The schism fuels a continuous class warfare, with a lower class struggling against the controlling groups, ultimately attaining their goals and then becoming the exploiters of yet another class. In this fashion, Marx outlined the emergence of the town-dwelling bourgeoisie of the Middle Ages, who successfully struggled against the feudal nobility and who, when they were finally in power, created the industrial state that then exploited the working class.

As Marx outlined the stages of revolutionary change in modern societies, the first step is the concentration of masses of workers in factory towns where they can exchange ideas and devise activist programmes through co-operation. As this co-operation grows, the workers become increasingly dissatisfied and ultimately reach a point at which they rebel and seize the means of production. Such revolutions demand the total destruction of the stratification system that preceded them, and also, Marx believed, the destruction of other aspects of the culture such as art, science and philosophy, which were created only to perpetuate the former ruling class.

Marx stated his view eloquently on the second page of the *Communist Manifesto:* "The history of all hitherto existing society is the history of class struggle. . . . The modern bourgeois society that has sprouted from the ruins of feudal society has not done away with class antagonisms. It has but established new classes, new conditions of oppression, new forms of struggle in place of the old ones. Our epoch, the epoch of the bourgeoisie, possesses, however, this distinctive feature: it has simplified the class antagonisms. Society as a whole is more and more splitting up into two great battle camps, into two great classes directly facing each other: bourgeoisie and proletariat."

The theories of both Marx and Durkheim can be used to explain social change, for both evolution and revolution accomplish fundamental alterations in conditions of life and attitudes towards it. In the dim past when human societies were first formed, they apparently lacked sharp divisions in status. Columbia University anthropologist Marvin Harris speculates that the dominant value in the Pleistocene era, when men were organized into simple hunting and gathering groups, was mainly egalitarian. Observing that similar groups surviving today divide the spoils of the hunt equally and share their scant resources with one another—rewards go to each individual according to his requirements, not according to his contributions to the group—Harris came to the conclusion that the classless society is in fact one of man's earliest. The

Flanked by dog guards, newly exalted pigs—the rulers in George Orwell's Animal Farm—*extract from rebellious hens confessions of wrongdoing. The illustration is from a 1954 animated cartoon that was based on the novel.*

A modern fable for revolutionists

The paradox of revolution—though it aims to eliminate privileges and status, it inevitably establishes new ones—was perhaps most sharply delineated by the English writer George Orwell in his now-classic 1946 satire, *Animal Farm*. In Orwell's brief novel, the protagonists are a group of barnyard animals. Led by the cleverest of their several species, the pigs, they expel their tyrannical human master, Farmer Jones. The pigs then proclaim all animals equal and organize them into a collective.

For a time, the new society works well. But one day the other animals find out that the pigs have been keeping the choicest food—milk and apples —for their own meals. Soon the pigs move from their sty to the farmhouse, empty since Jones's flight, explaining that as the managers of the farm they need a quiet place to work. Secluded behind its walls and guarded by a cadre of killer dogs, they institute an authoritarian regime, exterminating animals who oppose them, making the rest work long hours for short rations, and garnering the profits for themselves.

The farm's credo becomes "All animals are equal, but some animals are more equal than others". Those who formerly were oppressed have become the oppressors. In the book's final scene, the animals watch the pigs partying with visiting humans. Looking from pig to man and back again, they cannot tell which is which.

Though Orwell's satire was inspired directly by the Russian Revolution and Stalinist twisting of Marxist ideals, the author maintained that his intention was not to condemn or condone any political system. Rather, the book was intended as a warning of the corrupting influence of power, whether it is in traditional or revolutionary hands.

introduction of settled agriculture, however, created surplus resources, new specializations and a more complex social organization that offered the opportunity to compete for the means of production—both land and labour. With this increased competition, individuals attained greater rewards and power. During the process, people acquired a new value system that exalted the ability of individuals or groups to raise themselves above others.

A pioneer exponent of this view was archaeologist Karl Wittfogel, who linked the rise of the highly stratified early civilizations of ancient China, the Middle East and Peru to the introduction of irrigation. According to Wittfogel's "hydraulic theory" of civilization, irrigation works demanded new patterns of social organization that, among other things, required specialists and overseers to design the waterworks and to supervise the masses of labourers that were needed to build and maintain them. Efficient land and water management dictated larger landholdings, controlled by few but worked by many, which led ultimately to an upper stratum of powerful nobility, a middle range of traders for distribution, and a lower one of workers or slaves who were necessary to support the system.

This ancient scheme, a remarkably durable one, is called the traditional system of stratification. It is characteristic of agricultural societies where nearly everyone lives in villages and the dominant values are religious. Status is hereditary and regulated by law—the king's eldest son is destined to rule—and there are only a few levels in the stratification system, but subdivisions within the levels allow for remarkable variations. In old Russia, for example, serfs made up 80 per cent of the population and were at the bottom of the system. Some serfs went into trade and became wealthy businessmen, acquiring estates richer than those of many nobles; this economic advancement did not change their status as serfs, however, and legally they were subject to the same handicaps as their impoverished brethren.

Despite the rigidity of traditional status systems, they can be modified by a variety of political, social and economic influences and even by what seem to be acts of God. Shifts in birth and death rates or in migration patterns can have powerful but little-appreciated effects. The British historian J. H. Plumb traced a connection between the Black Death—the epidemic of bubonic plague that killed roughly one quarter of the population of Europe in the mid-14th century—and the rise of Renaissance craftsmen that occurred a hundred years later. According to Plumb, the Black Death so reduced the ranks of skilled craftsmen that the handiwork of the few survivors rose greatly in value. During the mercantile boom in Italy in the next few generations, such artifacts became prized symbols of status among rulers and Church princes: consequently, the artists grew increasingly wealthy, banding together into guilds that eventually became powerful social units in Florence, Venice and other centres of the Renaissance.

More commonly, however, status in traditional societies is altered by direct political action. Thus, Henry VIII in the 16th century could draw upon his aristocracy's discontent with the disproportionate wealth accumulated by the abbeys of the Roman Catholic Church and—with a single stroke of his pen—disestablish the Roman Catholic Church and later abolish the monasteries, thereby reducing once-lordly prelates to beggarly refugees.

Traditional societies in most parts of the world have now given way to those classified as modern. Their stratification systems contain many levels; movement from level to level is far easier than it was; the distinctions between the top and the bottom levels are far less; and within each level, status tends to be homogeneous—an elementary-schoolteacher performs much the same work the world over, and he is rewarded nearly everywhere with similar prestige, power and pay. Each level becomes more accessible to broad segments of the population. This homogeneous effect was noted even in the aristocratic Imperial Russian Army by Raymond L. Garthoff: "From 1861 to 1914 the continuing trend of the officer corps was evolution from partial and sometimes part-time service of a segment of the nobility toward a professionally and technically qualified group drawn from all classes". But, Garthoff added, the Czar attempted to maintain the form of the old aristocratic structure by granting "personal nobility" to everyone who was accepted as an officer—and those who made it to colonel were given hereditary nobility.

Such changes in status were forced on societies by technological innovation. Warfare came to require technically trained specialists of many kinds, and the nobility were neither numerous enough—nor, often, interested enough—to satisfy the need; armies had to recruit the talent they needed wherever it could be found. Technology and its partner, economics, have been responsible for drastically re-ordering status as societies that were structured along traditional lines have become modernized. Some positions, notably that of the clergy, were downgraded, while others—businessman, actor, banker, manufacturer, engineer—were elevated. But the principal effect has been to insert new rungs into the middle of the status ladder.

The invention of the steam railway in the early 19th century created the roles of conductor, driver, brakeman, signalman and many others.

Overpowered but unrepentant, a demonstrator for women's suffrage in England is led away from a horse race she tried to disrupt.

French women cram into a male-driven touring car in a suffrage campaign. They finally won in 1944.

A female fight for the rights of man

It took belligerent determination that was considered absent from "female character" to win women that basic element of status in the modern world, the right to vote. In England, members of the suffrage movement, begun in 1905, disrupted Parliament, harassed the Prime Minister and the King, and battled police all the way to jail, where their hunger strikes brought solitary confinement and brutal force feeding.

American women, taking the English crusade for a model, braved slaps and refuse thrown by hostile crowds to picket the White House in 1913. Those arrested later campaigned proudly in their prison uniforms. Such perseverance paid off. When the 20th century began, only New Zealand had given women the vote; by 1971, women voted in all but five of the world's leading countries.

A suffragette braves a male domain to peddle a feminist paper in a New York barber's shop. Though one state—Wyoming —gave women the vote in 1869, women's suffrage became nationwide only in 1920.

These positions were filled from the ranks of farm boys, servants and simple mechanics—in almost every case a step up to a status level not available before. A conductor, for example, stood above the closest comparable technician—a goods-train driver—because his job required more complex expertise and involved greater responsibility (a ship's captain continued to rank higher yet, however, because his job's demands were still greater).

In some cases, invention can lead to surprising changes in status. Men who dug ditches were once near the bottom of the stratification system. So low was their status that it was held up as a warning to boys who neglected their schoolwork: "Study," parents exhorted, "or you'll grow up to be a ditchdigger". Today most ditches are dug by machine. The contribution to society of the man who runs such a machine has changed little: ditches are still dug, but the occupation is now called machine operator; the pay is excellent, befitting an individual who is responsible for a complex and expensive device, and the status is accordingly much higher.

Yet something more than the practical considerations of technology and economics has been at work in the transition from traditional to modern status systems. People have altered the way they think about status, modifying their philosophical view of what is just and proper towards greater equality. This drive to lessen gross distinctions between lower levels and upper ones reinforces the pressures of industrialization, but it arose independently. Its ideas were formalized prior to the Industrial Revolution, principally in England and France in the 17th and 18th centuries by such philosophers as John Locke and Henry St. John, First Viscount of Bolingbroke. These views were first made official doctrine in the essentially agricultural society of Revolutionary America, when the Founding Fathers established an independent nation with the ringing assertion "that all men are created equal; that they are endowed by their creator with certain unalienable rights; that among these are life, liberty and the pursuit of happiness".

Such ideas affected even the most rigid of traditional systems. The Russia of Catherine the Great brooked no such nonsense as equal rights under law: the courts treated different classes differently. For example, corporal punishment was a sentence commonly imposed on everyone —except the nobility, who were specifically exempted. But in 1782 this right of exemption from whipping was extended to merchants, in 1863 to all inhabitants of towns, and, finally, to peasants. There was no clear economic necessity for these changes in the law; it was part of a worldwide transition towards modernism—"clear evidence", noted Alex Inkeles of Harvard University "of the diffusion of a status privilege initially

continued on page 161

Driving across the desert in his new car, a Saudi Arabian pulls up for a soft drink at a roadside stall. Cars became coveted status symbols in Arab countries, but the people were such careless drivers and there were so many new cars that in Kuwait one-third of the non-oil industry was devoted to car repairing.

A new class in the desert

When the price of oil soared during the energy crisis of the middle 1970s, the petroleum-producing Middle Eastern sheikdoms were the beneficiaries of what one commentator called "the greatest redistribution of wealth in history". The money came rolling in so fast that Saudi Arabia amassed a cash surplus of £12,000 million in a single year.

So great was the influx of new wealth that the entire status ladder was rearranged. Little of this wealth went directly into the pockets of individuals. Rather the money was put into government coffers and was used to raise the general standard of living. Saudi Arabia

opened a new school once every three days. In Kuwait, where there were only four doctors in 1952, the number rose to 800. Abu Dhabi constructed new housing for the Bedouins.

The benefits of these investments filtered down. People on the bottom rungs were lifted upwards by the rising tide of oil wealth. Arabs who had been leading a frugal existence suddenly were buying consumer goods: new cars, washing machines and colour television sets. A new status system, complete with middle and upper classes whose resources enabled them to enjoy Western-style luxuries, had been created.

*Saudi Arabian musicians play the
"hit parade" of Arab songs for television.
Once considered a "tool of the devil"
by religious leaders, TV became the only
accepted public entertainment.*

*In Saudi Arabia, where women still live
in the seclusion that is dictated by
Moslem law, two Saudi men inspect the
latest-model washing machines and
cookers in a well-stocked showroom.*

158

A veiled shopper browses through Paris originals in an Abu Dhabi boutique. Wealthy women wear such chic dresses under traditional robes and veils.

A sprawling new Islamic-style housing development rises in the desert near Kuwait City. In an effort to wipe out poverty, Kuwait is providing housing, jobs and education for every citizen.

Shoppers in Abu Dhabi try out an
ornate, rococo couch well suited to the
opulent Oriental rugs that are traditional
in this area—and to the ostentatious
houses built with riches derived from oil.

available to only the highest strata of society".

The combined effects of philosophy, technology and economics have by now brought more or less modern status systems to all parts of the world. Everywhere the trend has been towards egalitarianism, equal entitlement for everyone to "life, liberty and the pursuit of happiness". The results of such change are perhaps most noteworthy in three countries: the Soviet Union, China and Sweden.

In Russia, a rigid aristocratic system was turned upside down by means of a violent revolution, but the system was then replaced with a new order of elite classes that was scarcely less rigid than the old. In Sweden, rapid but peaceful political reform transformed what had been an essentially feudal structure into a modern society that is probably the most egalitarian in the world. In China, almost half a century of civil warfare brought to power a regime that seems to be determined to eliminate status completely, even at the cost of repeated upheaval, by forcing every one of its citizens—from university professors and government officials to peasant farmers and assembly-line workers—into a single class.

The Chinese effort to end class distinctions has been the most intense the world has yet seen. The Cultural Revolution—which, beginning in 1966, emptied the universities and government offices and sent intellectuals to work in fields and factories—is seen by the followers of Mao Tse-tung as a way of avoiding the tendency of human societies to create a new professional elite. They insist that peasants and workers can learn technical skills and run the government, bringing to their tasks the proletarian outlook that was lacking in their predecessors. The Maoists believe a continuing process of indoctrination and self-criticism will ensure that these newly elevated peasants and workers do not waver from proletarian ideals.

The success of the Chinese experiment cannot be measured for decades. But the possibility of achieving a considerable degree of egalitarianism in a fairly brief period—by reform rather than revolution —has been demonstrated in Sweden.

In the middle of the 19th century, the Swedish kingdom was a rigidly stratified relic of feudal times: landed gentry, the clergy and urban burghers held undisputed power over a far more populous peasantry that was engaged principally in farming. Although there was some industry—logging, and iron and copper mining—it, too, was feudal in structure, organized in *bruks*, isolated communities in which the relationship between workers and owner-managers resembled that between serfs and lords of mediaeval estates.

"Poverty, overcrowding, starvation and sickness," wrote Swedish scholar Ake Elmer, "were common in Sweden around the turn of the century. And in contrast to this there was an upper class, which in magnificence and wealth stood far above the great mass of people. An intermediate level was made up of the propertied farmer class, the lower-middle-class craftsmen and merchants, and the beginnings of a white-collar class, each group of which looked down upon the others, but all of whom were objects of contempt to the upper class and envy to the working class."

This oppressive class structure drove many Swedes to emigrate—an estimated million went to the United States alone between 1860 and 1910. One emigrant, recalling a near-starving 78-hour-a-week apprenticeship in Sweden, wrote of his co-workers: "I have seen slaves since in Africa and Australia, and they were treated better". A woman wrote,

"I could cry when I remember how it was. We servants were all like slaves and were so happy when we weren't scolded".

That such a harshly divided status system could be wiped out within a few decades is surprising enough, but that the transformation could be accomplished as calmly as it was may be even more striking. The development of manufacturing and great expansion in timber, paper and steel industries brought new riches to Sweden and led the lower classes to demand a bigger share not only of money but also of everything that goes with it—education, housing, medical care, honours and political power. The upper classes did not resist very strongly, apparently because of "the tranquil Swedish character", according to an American journalist David Jenkins. Commenting on modern Sweden, he maintained: "The tranquillity is not a result of this streamlined modern system (as anyone can verify by reading the comments of foreign travellers in the eighteenth or nineteenth century); it is one of the creative forces behind the system. Only by being calm, unemotional, and coldly rational could the Swedes have avoided the rancorous conflicts that have torn so many countries apart".

There was exactly one general strike, in 1909, during the course of the half-century reorganization of the Swedish social structure. The most infamous incident of violence, known as the Adalen Massacre, was a 1931 battle between strikers and police in which four workers and a 10-year-old girl were killed. Memories of this event still trouble most Swedes, although it hardly compares with the strife that killed 1,300 people in Spain in 1934 or with the murderous guerrilla warfare involving the coal miners of Harlan County in Kentucky. The Adalen Massacre impelled the Swedes to seek—and to find—consensus, expressed in the expanding system of social welfare that eventually wiped out most distinctions among its citizens.

There is still a ladder of status in Sweden, but the differences between the rungs now are not great, and they depend mostly on fine points of power and prestige. Legal rights, general respect and adequate living standards are available to everyone. "It requires some ingenuity to escape a comfortable existence," reported the British journalist Roland Huntford. This "comfortable existence" is assured by taxation that takes money from the people at the upper levels and redistributes it among those at the lower levels in the form of free medical care, large pensions, allowances for the care and education of children, state housing, tuition-free universities and a host of other social services (for instance, housewives are entitled to government-paid holidays). The income tax is steeply progressive—in the mid-1970s, a family with an income of £12,000 had to give £6,000 of it back in income taxes, whereas a sim-

Dunces caps and placards make Chinese railway officials ridiculous in 1967 during the Cultural Revolution, a calculated effort to level status by discrediting an elite of experts who held influential jobs.

Seeking a status that society denied them, homosexuals stage a protest march in New York City. They sought equality with the heterosexual majority in the early 1970s by forming militant organizations such as the Gay Activists Alliance, which pressed for laws that would prohibit discrimination against them in housing and job opportunities.

ilarly situated family in the United States would be required to pay only about £2,500 in taxes.

With this levelling of income comes a levelling of behaviour. Speech and accents depend little on social status, in sharp contrast to the profoundly significant variations in Britain and the United States. The same is true of dress; everyone wears much the same style of clothing, and when a cleaning woman comes to the house she generally arrives formally dressed and changes for work. Even reading habits are remarkably uniform. Sweden supports the largest per capita circulation of newspapers in the world, and nearly everyone reads both the serious and sensational publications. According to a study that was published in 1965, working-class Swedes read an average of 1.53 newspapers a day, somewhat more than people of the rural middle class and only slightly less than the urban middle class. Even voting is less influenced by status level than it is in other countries. An analysis of the 1964 election showed that, in the highest status level, 91 per cent voted, compared

Seeking to maintain their status, London market workers protest about the arrival of 50,000 Asians expelled from Uganda in 1972. The Britons, carrying posters to indicate support of the anti-immigration stand of political leader Enoch Powell, feared the immigrants would take their jobs away and weaken their already insecure hold on middle-class rank.

to 87 per cent for the lowest level, a difference of just 4 percentage points; a similar study that was conducted in the United States found a difference of 16 percentage points between the highest and the lowest levels of the population.

But egalitarianism has not brought happiness. In 1958 the Swedish opinion-research group called SIFO surveyed a representative sample of 750 Swedes; surprisingly, the researchers found that only 47 per cent of the Swedes they questioned named their own country as the one in which "people are happiest" (36 per cent responded that there is no such country). Rising discontent has focused on the high cost of the social welfare system, on the limitations on the control of the individual over his own destiny, and on the power that is wielded by those who administer public policy. For if everyone is nearly equal in Sweden, some people are still more equal than others.

One of the most important factors that determines a Swede's prestige is occupation (*page 46*). University professors are rated highest, and for some reason that baffles sociologists, all other teachers are close behind, ranked higher than they are in many other countries. An odd reflection of this concern with occupation as the mark of prestige is visible in Swedish telephone directories, in which people are listed first according to their jobs, address or other category, and only then by their names. In order to look up Carl Johansson it is first necessary to know whether he is an architect or a journalist—a requirement that is only partly explained by the fact that the Stockholm telephone directory contains more than 50 pages of Johanssons. Aristocratic lineage may still be very important privately, but publicly it is studiously ignored; the head of the Nobel Foundation, for example, is always referred to as Mr. Ramel, not Baron Ramel.

The great esteem that is accorded educated intellectuals does not, of itself, confer equivalent power. The government has been controlled largely by the labour unions, which collaborate with organizations representing other interests in a way that has led to the concentration of economic power within the confines of a small elite group. Fifteen families, together with two corporations, control concerns that employ almost half of all the workers in private industry. Yet by the standards of other countries the elite families of Sweden are not super-rich. The most powerful of them, the Wallenbergs (SKF ball bearings, Saab cars and Ericsson telephones, among some 70 businesses), have a combined private fortune that is on a par with the lowest levels of wealthy families in the United States.

While Sweden's peaceful evolution did not create a totally classless society, that was never the stated goal. "Wealth is okay," maintained a left-wing socialist in a high government post in 1976, "if it is invested in a way useful to society." A quite opposite case history can be found in the Soviet Union. There total egalitarianism was indeed the aim of the 1917 Revolution, which was supposed to employ class warfare to eliminate classes. It did not work out that way.

The restructuring of the Russian status system was achieved during a period of violence and destruction that almost wrecked the country. An estimated 8.5 million people died, one million of them in fighting that did not end until 1922, the rest in epidemics and famines. The first concern of the Soviet leaders was the complete destruction of the old order, and they reversed the imperial status ladder. At the top was the Communist Party itself. But next, in order, came manual labourers, landless peasants, clerks, "working" intelligentsia (such as technicians and teachers) and the better-off peasants. At the bottom of the ladder was the old elite: nobles, officials, merchants, landowners and priests. "The strata were legally defined," according to Alex Inkeles of Harvard University, "and frequently enjoyed markedly different privileges, as in the allotment of housing and ration cards. Their obligations also varied. The former exploiting classes were to be called on first for such duties as street cleaning."

This inverted ladder was seen as a preliminary move toward an egalitarian society in which everyone would have much the same status. But workers and peasants did not last for long on the top rung of the Soviet ladder. By the 1930s, the demands of economic development for trained specialists of all kinds forced a change to status that was based on achievement. In 1931, Stalin attacked "equality-mongering", and set up "a system of payment that gives each worker his due according to his qualifications". The result of this system has been a social structure that is divided into several major classes, with the expert bureaucrats and technicians at the top and the workers and peasants near the bottom. The various classes were initially accessible to all, but mobility —while still great—has recently been limited as the upper classes not only accumulated wealth and privilege but also found ways to entrench their positions.

The principal route up in the Soviet Union, as elsewhere in the modern world, is through education. And access to high-quality education became easier for children of the elite, more difficult for children of the lower classes. In selecting boys for military schools, preference was given to sons of high-ranking officers. Stiff academic requirements for admission to universities served to eliminate most applicants who had not had the advantage of an upper-class upbringing—good elementary schools and the rich cultural environment provided by an educated family. As a result, the children of the urban intelligentsia are at least 16 times more likely to acquire higher education than are the children of peasants, according to Zev Katz of Massachusetts Institute of Technology. Even in small towns, similar distinctions were found, he wrote. "A study of the average length of schooling received by children in the towns of Ufa and Orenburg, for example, showed that children of peasant families received an average of 7.31 years of schooling, the children of working-class families 7.66 years, and the children of the intelligentsia (broadly defined to include all non-manuals) 12.22 years."

Thus the Soviet Union, which once had seemed intent on glorifying the worker, came to glorify the manager. Of 121 Stalin Prizes that were awarded in 1948 for industrial innovations, only five went to people who might be considered workers; all the rest were granted to engineers, scientists and managers. Of perhaps more importance to the establishment of a permanent elite were changes in the distribution of

*London crowds watch Elizabeth II's coronation
procession in 1953. The pomp associated with her rank
survives despite the weakening of the monarchy.*

economic rewards. The tax rates were reduced on the higher brackets of income—at one point a tenfold increase in income involved only a doubling in the total tax paid (in the United States, by contrast, a jump from a £6,000 annual salary to £60,000 would multiply the income tax 18 times). Not only were individuals enabled to accumulate wealth in their lifetimes, but they were also given ways of passing it along to their descendants. Death duties were sharply reduced, and special pensions were granted; Alex Inkeles reported, among other examples, that in 1946 "the widow of Lieutenant General of Engineering Troops D. M. Karbyshev was granted a pension of 1,000 roubles a month, and his daughter and son each 700 roubles per month until the completion of their education".

In these ways, elitism and stratification manage to survive or re-emerge in most countries despite the most determined revolutionary or reformist movements. In England, Parliamentary acts have tried to dismantle great fortunes, end inherited wealth and demolish the country's hoary class system. But the image of the impoverished gentry and a declining upper class is largely just that—an image. The British author Anthony Sampson noted: "The aristocracy are, in general, much richer than they seem. With democracy has come discretion. Their London palaces and outward show have disappeared, but the countryside is still full of millionaire peers: many of them, with the boom in property, are richer now than they ever have been. . . . Members of some of the oldest families are still among the richest men in Britain. Death duties, which used to eat into the large fortunes, are now nearly always circumvented by trusts and gifts." The French sociologist Raymond Aron called the persistent British stratification "the best example of a country whose regime is Western but which still possesses a ruling class: the higher echelons in the world of affairs, of the university, of the press, church, and of politics find themselves in the same clubs; they often have family ties, they are aware of the community they constitute".

Such status differences have also been exported via colonialism, and they persist long after the colony has become independent. Anthropologist Leonard Plotnicov reported that the central Nigerian city of Jos possessed a new elite that is "recognized by their modern and prestigeful occupations and greater wealth" and also by their propensity for all things European. This new high status group spoke cultured —even Victorian—English with no tinge of an African accent; preferred European drink, food and dress; employed elaborate social etiquette; and frequented elaborate country clubs where one of the favourite sports was lawn tennis. Members of this group—which included government officials, school directors and managers of large firms—

attended the cinema only on "European nights", when admission prices were raised to keep out the poor and illiterate Nigerian workers who attended on other evenings.

The fact that stratification is so universal and enduring suggests to some social scientists that status differences are necessary components of every social structure. Sociologist Robert Bierstedt has contended that status is necessary to establish clear lines of authority. Every organization, he suggests, must designate who gives the orders and who obeys if the group is to function at all.

Two other sociologists, Kingsley Davis and Wilbert Moore, probed the origins of status differences. The function of status, they concluded, is to entice individuals to fill such positions. To do this may require many long years of training and sacrifice, and then arduous labour to satisfy the demands of a position. A physician, for example, must undergo costly, difficult schooling and then—at least in theory—be pre-pared to offer his services whenever needed. According to Davis and Moore, society induces people to undertake such hardships by offering them high status, wealth and esteem—badges of honour associated with the medical profession in most societies.

To get the right people into the right social slots, Davis and Moore theorized, "society must have, first, some kinds of rewards that it can use as inducements, and, second, some way of distributing these rewards according to positions. The rewards and their distribution become part of the social order and thus give rise to stratification."

Davis and Moore divided the rewards available into three categories: things that contribute to sustenance and comfort; things that contribute to humour and diversion; and, finally, things that contribute to self-respect and "ego expansion".

While many sociologists disagree with Davis and Moore about the necessity of both stratification and special rewards, the persistence of both, particularly in systems that are based on Marxist ideals of egali-tarianism, is as notable today as it was in the time of Alphonse Karr. In the Soviet Union, for example, leaders of the Communist Party, top scientists, artists and bureaucrats draw their elegant imported foodstuffs from specially stocked state shops free of charge; the average Russian working family, on the other hand, spends up to half its monthly income on groceries. The privileged can import from abroad limousines and sports cars. In cities in which there are chronic housing shortages, the new Communist aristocrats are often given spacious flats fitted with foreign-made appliances and furnishings that have been imported from abroad. In the countryside, their residences are sometimes even more lavish: palaces, newly built or survivals from the czarist period, that are staffed by well-trained discreet servants.

Muscovites find this high living such a mockery of Soviet ideals that there was a standing joke about the Party boss Leonid Brezhnev. According to the story—told in the book *The Russians*, by Hedrick Smith, long the *New York Times* correspondent in Moscow—Brezhnev wanted to impress his mother with how well he had done. He invited her to Moscow to show her around his luxurious flat. But she seemed ill at ease, so he whisked her in a limousine out to his enormous *dacha*, a country estate formerly used by Stalin and Khrushchev, and took her on a tour of the elegantly appointed rooms and extensive grounds. When she still had no comment, he ordered his private helicopter and flew her off to his hunting lodge, showing off the banqueting room, his guns and trophies. But when she still did not speak, he could no longer restrain himself. "Tell me, Mama," he asked at last. "What do you think?"

"Well," she said hesitantly. "It's good, Leonid. But what if the Reds come back?"

Acknowledgements

The index for this book was prepared by Elizabeth C. Graham. The author and editors of this book are particularly indebted to Professor A. H. Halsey, Department of Social and Administrative Studies, University of Oxford, England. They also wish to thank the following persons and institutions: Dr. Heribert Becher, Sociological Institute, University of Bonn, Germany; Philippe Droin, Chargé de Mission Auprès de Président de L'Association des Anciens Sciences Po, Paris; Harold Ellis, Professor of Surgery, University of London; Enid Farmer, Lexington, Massachusetts; Mariella Ferrari, C.I.G.A., Rome; Liz Goodman, London; John Halas, Halas and Batchelor Animation Film, Ltd., London; René Henry-Gréard, Secrétaire Général de L'Institut D'Etudes Politiques de Paris; Gastone Marri, Director, C.R.D., Federazione Unitaria Sindacale, Rome; David Martin, Professor of Sociology, London School of Economics; Francesco Novara, Director, Psychological Research, Olivetti S.P.A., Ivrea, Italy; Philippe Rossi, Paris; Giorgio Tommaseo-Ponzetta, C.I.G.A., Venice, Italy; Michel Weulersse, Paris; Jan Yoors, New York City.

Bibliography

Becker, Howard S., *Outsiders, Studies in the Sociology of Deviance*. The Free Press, 1963.

Bendix, Reinhard, and Seymour Martin Lipset, eds., *Class, Status, and Power: Social Stratification in Comparative Perspective*. The Free Press, 1966.

Berger, Peter L. and Brigitte, *Sociology: A Biographical Approach*. Basic Books, Inc., 1975.

Bex, Maurice, *Manet*. Continental Book Center, Inc., 1948.

Blau, Peter, and Otis Dudley Duncan, *The American Occupational Structure*. John Wiley & Sons, Inc., 1967.

Bredemeier, Harry C., and Jackson Toby, *Social Problems in America*. John Wiley & Sons, Inc., 1972.

Clébert, Jean-Paul, *The Gypsies*. Translated by Charles Duff. Vista Books, 1963.

Coxon, A. P. M., and C. L. Jones, *Social Mobility*. Penguin Books, 1975.

Duret, Theodore, *Manet*. Crown Publishers, 1937.

Freedman, Jonathan L., and Anthony N. Doob, *Deviancy, The Psychology of Being Different*. Academic Press, 1968.

Giddens, Anthony, *The Class Structure of the Advanced Societies*. Hutchinson Education, 1973.

Hall, John, and Caradog Jones, "Social Grading of Occupations," *The British Journal of Sociology*, Vol. 1, no. 1, 1950.

Halsey, A. H., Jean Floud and C. Arnold Anderson, *Education, Economy and Society*. The Free Press, 1965.

Hamilton, George Heard, *Manet and His Critics*. Yale University Press, 1954.

Harris, Marvin, *Rise of Anthropological Theory: A History of Theories of Culture*. Routledge and Kegan Paul, 1969.

Himmelfarb, Gertrude, *Darwin and the Darwinian Revolution*. Doubleday Anchor Books, 1959.

Hodge, Robert W., Paul M. Siegel, and Peter H. Rossi, "Occupational Prestige in the United States: 1925-1963," *American Journal of Sociology*, no. 70, 1964.

Hodges, Harold M., Jr., *Social Stratification: Class in America*. Schenkman Publishing Co., 1964.

Hoebel, E. Adamson, *The Cheyennes, Indians of the Great Plains*. Henry Holt and Company, 1960.

Houriet, Robert, *Getting Back Together*. Sphere Books, 1973.

Hutton, J. H., *Caste in India*. Oxford University Press, 1963.

Inkeles, Alex, *Social Change in Soviet Russia*. Harvard University Press, 1968.

Jencks, Christopher, *Inequality*. Penguin Books, 1975.

Jenkins, David, *Sweden and the Price of Progress*. Coward, McCann & Geoghegan, Inc., 1968.

Jones, Edward E., and Harold B. Gerard, *Foundations of Social Psychology*. John Wiley & Sons, Inc., 1967.

Kohn, Melvin L., *Class and Conformity: A Study in Values*. The Dorsey Press, 1969.

Lemert, Edwin M., *Social Pathology*. McGraw-Hill Book Company, Inc., 1951.

Linton, Ralph, *The Tree of Culture*. Vintage Books, 1973.

Lipset, Seymour M., and Reinhard Bendix, *Social Mobility in Industrial Society*. University of California Press, 1965.

London, Perry, and David Rosenhan, ed., *Foundations of Abnormal Psychology*. Holt, Rinehart and Winston, Inc., 1968.

McClelland, David C., *The Achieving Society*. The Free Press, 1967.

Mayer, Kurt B., and Walter Buckley, *Class and Society*. Random House, 1969.

Merton, Robert K., *Social Theory and Social Structure*. The Free Press of Glencoe, 1968.

Mitford, Nancy, ed., *Noblesse Oblige*. Hamish Hamilton Ltd., London, 1973.

Sitwell, Edith, *English Eccentrics*. Penguin Books, 1971.

Smith, Hedrick, *The Russians.* Quadrangle/ The New York Times Book Co., 1976.

Sorokin, Pitirim A., *Social and Cultural Mobility.* The Free Press, 1959.

Sutherland, Anne, *Gypsies: The Hidden Americans.* Tavistock Publications, 1975.

Thoreau, Henry D., *Walden.* Collier-Mac-millan, 1962.

Tomasson, Richard F., *Sweden: Prototype of Modern Society.* Random House, 1970.

Vallentin, Antonina, *The Drama of Albert Einstein.* Doubleday & Company, Inc., 1954.

The Vogue Book of Etiquette. Simon & Schuster, 1948.

Warner, W. Lloyd, *Yankee City.* Yale University Press, 1963.

Yoors, Jan, *The Gypsies.* Simon & Schuster, 1967.

Zinkin, Taya, *Caste Today.* Oxford University Press, 1962.

Picture Credits

Index

Numerals in italics indicate a photograph or drawing of the subject mentioned.

✗Filmsetting by C: E. Dawkins (Typesetter) Ltd., London, SE1 1UN.
Printed and bound in Spain by Novograph, S.A.
D. L.: M-27503-1977